Introduction to Personal Computers Using Windows® 7

Introduction to Personal Computers Using Windows® 7

Part Number: 084705
Course Edition: 1.0

NOTICES

DISCLAIMER: While Element K Corporation takes care to ensure the accuracy and quality of these materials, we cannot guarantee their accuracy, and all materials are provided without any warranty whatsoever, including, but not limited to, the implied warranties of merchantability or fitness for a particular purpose. The name used in the data files for this course is that of a fictitious company. Any resemblance to current or future companies is purely coincidental. We do not believe we have used anyone's name in creating this course, but if we have, please notify us and we will change the name in the next revision of the course. Element K is an independent provider of integrated training solutions for individuals, businesses, educational institutions, and government agencies. Use of screenshots, photographs of another entity's products, or another entity's product name or service in this book is for editorial purposes only. No such use should be construed to imply sponsorship or endorsement of the book by, nor any affiliation of such entity with Element K. This courseware may contain links to sites on the Internet that are owned and operated by third parties (the "External Sites"). Element K is not responsible for the availability of, or the content located on or through, any External Site. Please contact Element K if you have any concerns regarding such links or External Sites.

TRADEMARK NOTICES Element K and the Element K logo are trademarks of Element K Corporation and its affiliates.

Windows® 7 is a registered trademark of Microsoft Corporation in the U.S. and other countries; the Microsoft products and services discussed or described may be trademarks of Microsoft Corporation. All other product names and services used throughout this course may be common law or registered trademarks of their respective proprietors.

Copyright © 2009 Element K Corporation. All rights reserved. Screenshots used for illustrative purposes are the property of the software proprietor. This publication, or any part thereof, may not be reproduced or transmitted in any form or by any means, electronic or mechanical, including photocopying, recording, storage in an information retrieval system, or otherwise, without express written permission of Element K, 500 Canal View Boulevard, Rochester, NY 14623, (585) 240-7500, (800) 478-7788. Element K Courseware's World Wide Web site is located at **www.elementkcourseware.com**.

This book conveys no rights in the software or other products about which it was written; all use or licensing of such software or other products is the responsibility of the user according to terms and conditions of the owner. Do not make illegal copies of books or software. If you believe that this book, related materials, or any other Element K materials are being reproduced or transmitted without permission, please call (800) 478-7788.

HELP US IMPROVE OUR COURSEWARE

Your comments are important to us. Please contact us at Element K Press LLC, 1-800-478-7788, 500 Canal View Boulevard, Rochester, NY 14623, Attention: Product Planning, or through our Web site at **http://support.elementkcourseware.com**.

Introduction to Personal Computers Using Windows® 7

Lesson 1: Getting Started with Personal Computers

    A. Identify Personal Computer Basics 2

    B. Identify Input Devices 9

    C. Identify Output Devices. 15

    D. Identify Storage Devices 22

    E. Set Up the Computer 26

    F. Examine Personal Computer Functionality 31

Lesson 2: Exploring Windows 7 Operating System

    A. Log On to Windows 7 Operating System 40

    B. Explore the Desktop 52

    C. Work with Windows 58

    D. Use Windows Help and Support 67

    E. Turn Off Personal Computers 71

Lesson 3: Managing Folders and Files

    A. Navigate to Folders with Windows Explorer 78

    B. Work with Folders and Files 88

    C. Copy Data on Storage Media. 100

Lesson 4: Using Common Tools and Programs

    A. Examine Application Software 106

    B. Create a Document in WordPad 110

    C. Work with the Calculator 117

D. Customize a Graphic with the Paint Tool 122

Lesson 5: Customizing the Windows 7 Desktop

A. Customize the Start Menu 130

B. Customize the Taskbar 135

C. Personalize the Desktop 141

D. Set a Screen Saver 149

E. Add Gadgets 154

Lesson 6: Browsing the Internet

A. An Overview of Networks 162

B. Browse Websites with Internet Explorer 8 165

Lesson Labs 179

Solutions 187

Glossary 201

Index 209

About This Course

To keep pace with today's fast moving business environment, you need to create, maintain, and share large volumes of information. Completing these tasks manually might be time-consuming and unprofitable. Computers are the prerequisite to ensure that business information is stored, processed, and delivered with speed and accuracy. This course will provide you with the basic skills needed to get started with personal computers and work with the various features, tools, and options available in Windows 7. In this course, you will familiarize yourself with the basics of personal computers, customize Windows 7, and manage files and folders. You will also work with simple tools and browse the Internet.

In a fast-moving business environment, where almost everything revolves around personal computers, everyone needs to understand computers and work with them. But computers are not just for business users; many individuals today own computers for private use. Acquiring computer skills or updating your existing ones is important whether you are a new job seeker, a private individual with a computer at home, or an established professional seeking to grow along your current career path.

Course Description

Target Student

This course is targeted to individuals who do not have any background, knowledge, or experience in computers and who need to use personal computers at home or the office.

Course Prerequisites

There are no prerequisites required for this course.

How to Use This Book

As a Learning Guide

Each lesson covers one broad topic or set of related topics. Lessons are arranged in order of increasing proficiency with *Introduction to Personal Computers Using Windows® 7*; skills you acquire in one lesson are used and developed in subsequent lessons. For this reason, you should work through the lessons in sequence.

We organized each lesson into results-oriented topics. Topics include all the relevant and supporting information you need to master *Introduction to Personal Computers Using Windows® 7*, and activities allow you to apply this information to practical hands-on examples.

You get to try out each new skill on a specially prepared sample file. This saves you typing time and allows you to concentrate on the skill at hand. Through the use of sample files, hands-on activities, illustrations that give you feedback at crucial steps, and supporting background information, this book provides you with the foundation and structure to learn *Introduction to Personal Computers Using Windows® 7* quickly and easily.

As a Review Tool

Any method of instruction is only as effective as the time and effort you are willing to invest in it. In addition, some of the information that you learn in class may not be important to you immediately, but it may become important later on. For this reason, we encourage you to spend some time reviewing the topics and activities after the course. For additional challenge when reviewing activities, try the "What You Do" column before looking at the "How You Do It" column.

As a Reference

The organization and layout of the book make it easy to use as a learning tool and as an after-class reference. You can use this book as a first source for definitions of terms, background information on given topics, and summaries of procedures.

Course Icons

Icon	Description
	A **Caution Note** makes students aware of potential negative consequences of an action, setting, or decision that are not easily known.
	Display Slide provides a prompt to the instructor to display a specific slide. Display Slides are included in the Instructor Guide only.
	An **Instructor Note** is a comment to the instructor regarding delivery, classroom strategy, classroom tools, exceptions, and other special considerations. Instructor Notes are included in the Instructor Guide only.
	Notes Page indicates a page that has been left intentionally blank for students to write on.
	A **Student Note** provides additional information, guidance, or hints about a topic or task.
	A **Version Note** indicates information necessary for a specific version of software.

Course Objectives

In this course, you will familiarize yourself with the basic components of personal computers, log on to Windows 7, explore the Windows 7 interface, manage files and folders, use the common tools and programs available in Windows 7, customize the Windows 7 desktop, and browse the Internet.

You will:

- examine the parts that make up a personal computer to familiarize yourself with the basic components and individual functions of each component.
- explore the Windows 7 operating system after logging on to it using the personal computer.
- manage files and folders using Windows Explorer to navigate to folders and manage files.
- understand application software, and use common tools and applications that are part of the Windows 7 operating system such as the WordPad word processor, the Paint tool, the Calculator tool, among others.
- customize the Windows 7 desktop using the customizing tools and shortcuts to personalize the desktop to suit your business requirements.

- examine networking tools and features so that you can browse for information using the Internet.

Course Requirements

Hardware

This course requires one desktop computer for each student.

- Intel® Pentium® IV 800 MHz or higher
- Minimum 512MB of RAM or higher
- 128 MB graphics processor that supports DirectX® 9.0
- Generic Monitor (1024x768)
- 16 GB hard disk space for 32 bit or 20 GB hard disk space for 64 bit
- DVD R/RW drive
- High-speed Internet connection
- A few recordable CDs/DVDs

Software

- Microsoft® Windows® 7
- DirectX® 9.0

Class Setup

Install Windows 7 Ultimate Edition

To install Windows 7 Ultimate edition:

1. Boot your computer with the DVD containing Ultimate Edition.
2. In the **Install Windows** window, click **Next** to continue the setup.
3. Click the **Install Now** button.
4. Accept the license agreement and click **Next** to continue.
5. On the **Which type of installation do you want** screen, select **Custom (Advanced)**.
6. In the **Where do you want to install Windows** window, create two partitions (C and D) with a minimum capacity of 20 GB and 10 GB, respectively. Format the partitions to NTFS.
7. Select the C drive partition to install Windows 7 and click **Next** to continue.
8. The computer will automatically restart after a few minutes. Remove the DVD before the system restarts.
9. After finalizing the setup, the computer will restart once again.
10. In the **Type a user name** text box, enter a account name of Student##, where ## is a unique number between 1 and 10. Name the instructor's user account Student00.
11. If necessary, in the **Type a computer name** text box, type a computer name.
12. In the **Type a password** text box, type *p@ssw0rd*

13. In the **Retype a password** text box, retype the password to confirm the login details.
14. In the **Type a password hint** text box, type *p@ssw0rd* and click **Next** to continue.
15. In the **Product Key** text box, type the product key of your software and click **Next** to continue.
16. On the **Help protect windows automatically** screen, click **Use recommended settings.**
17. Specify your time and date settings.
    - From the **Time zone** drop-down list, select your time zone.
    - In the **Date** section, select the date.
    - If necessary, modify the system time.
18. Click **Next** to continue.
19. On the **Select your computer's current location** screen, click **Work network.**

Configure the Internet Settings

1. Choose **Start→Control Panel→Network and Internet.**
2. Click **Internet Options** to open the **Internet Properties** dialog box.
3. On the **General** tab, in the **Home Page** section, click **Use Blank.**
4. If necessary, on the **Connections** tab, configure the network connection settings as appropriate for your network environment.
5. Click **Apply** and then click **OK.**

Configure Default Internet Settings in Internet Explorer 8

1. Run Internet Explorer.
2. In the **Set Up Windows Internet Explorer 8** wizard, on the **Welcome to Internet Explorer 8** page, click **Next.**
3. On the **Turn on Suggested Sites** page, select **Yes, turn on Suggested Sites** and click **Next.**
4. On the **Choose your settings** page, select the **Choose custom settings** option and click **Next.**
5. On the **Choose a default search provider** page, verify that the default search provider is **Bing Search** and select the **Keep my current default search provider** option and click **Next.**
6. On the **Choose your Accelerators providers** page, select the **Keep my current Accelerators** option and click **Next.**
7. On the **Turn on SmartScreen Filter** page, verify that the **Turn on SmartScreen Filter (recommended)** option is selected and click **Next.**
8. On the **Compatibility Settings** page, select the **Yes, I want to use updates** option and click **Finish.**
9. If necessary, connect to a website to ensure that all computers in the classroom have access to the Internet.
10. Close Internet Explorer.
11. Choose **Start→Shut down options→Log Off.**

Disable the AutoPlay Feature

1. Choose **Start→Control Panel→All Control Panel Items→AutoPlay.**

If your book did not come with a CD, please go to **http://www.elementk.com/courseware-file-downloads** to download the data files.

2. In the **AutoPlay** window, uncheck the **Use AutoPlay for all media and devices** check box.
3. Click **Save.**

Initial Class Setup

1. On the course CD-ROM, double-click the **084705exe** self-extracting file. This will install a folder named 084705Data on your C drive. This folder contains all the data files that you will use to complete this course.
2. Navigate to the C:\084705Data folder and copy the subfolders within the Datafiles folder to the root of the D drive.
3. In addition to the specific setup procedures needed for this class to run properly, you should also check the Element K Press product support website at **http://support.elementkcourseware.com** for more information. Any update about this course will be posted there.

List of Additional Files

Printed with each activity is a list of files students open to complete that activity. Many activities also require additional files that students do not open, but are needed to support the file(s) students are working with. These supporting files are included with the student data files on the course CD-ROM or data disk. Do not delete these files.

1 | Getting Started with Personal Computers

Lesson Time: 35 minutes

Lesson Objectives:

In this lesson, you will examine the parts that make up a personal computer to familiarize yourself with the basic components and individual functions of each component.

You will:

- Identify the types of personal computers to familiarize yourself with their uses and functions.
- Describe the input devices so that you can feed input to the computer.
- Identify output devices that are used to communicate digital information to the user.
- Describe the different storage devices that help to store information.
- Identify ways to set up the computer to start using it.
- Examine the personal computer's functionality to identify the common functions and processes of operations.

Introduction

You are new to computers and will be using Microsoft® Windows® 7. The first step is to gain a solid foundation of computer basics. In this lesson, you will examine the basics of personal computers.

Today, personal computers have become an integral part of our lives. Be it at the office or at home, most of our communication with the world around us takes place with the help of these personal computers. Whether you already own and use a computer or are looking to buy one, getting acquainted with the basics of personal computers will help you use them effectively.

TOPIC A
Identify Personal Computer Basics

More than likely, you know people who use personal computers, and subsequently you want to use one. Before you use a personal computer, it is essential that you do some groundwork on what personal computers can help you do. In this topic, you will identify a personal computer and its many uses.

Currently, personal computers, or PCs, play a vital role in diversified fields. Given the widespread use of personal computers, you may want to explore how a personal computer can aid you with your work and personal needs. Identifying the features, functions, and the potential uses of a PC will help you get the most out of your computer.

Personal Computers

Definition:

A *computer* is a fast operating, versatile machine that stores, retrieves, and processes data. It contains various electronic components, generically referred to as *hardware*. It follows a specific set of electronic instructions, called *software*. A *personal computer*, or *microcomputer*, is a small size computer that typically is designed to be used by one person at a time for programs that require relatively little computing power. Personal computers are available in various sizes and models, depending on the specific use it is put to and the needs of the user.

Example:

Figure 1-1: A personal computer that is used to store, retrieve, and process data.

Types of Personal Computers

There are different types of personal computers, and it is important to use the one that best fits your working style and needs. The following table provides a description of each of the types.

Computer Type	Description
Desktop	 A personal computer designed to be used on your desk at home or office. It is not meant to be portable. It usually includes a tower-style system unit with an external keyboard, a monitor, and a mouse. Typically, a desktop is the most powerful of all the types of personal computers because it can be easily upgraded by adding or replacing components. Desktops tend to offer the most features for your money. Key attributes include power, performance, and upgradeability. Some examples of desktop PC manufacturers include Apple, Dell, and Hewlett-Packard.

Computer Type	Description
Laptop	 A personal computer that integrates the system unit, monitor, keyboard, and mouse available with a desktop computer into one portable package. Laptops ordinarily weigh between four and eight pounds and are designed to be carried and used in locations outside the home or office. They can either be plugged into an electrical outlet or battery operated. Laptop computers typically have less processing power and fewer features than desktops. They also tend to be more expensive and less upgradeable than desktop computers. Key attributes include a nice combination of functionality and freedom to work in different locations. Companies that make desktops also manufacture laptops.

Computer Type	Description
Handheld	 A computer designed to fit in your hand. This is the smallest type of personal computer making it easy to carry anywhere. Handhelds are battery-operated with targeted but limited capabilities. Usually, a small keyboard or a pen-like stylus is used to operate a handheld. You cannot perform all types of tasks on a handheld computer that you can perform on a desktop or notebook computer. However, handhelds function well as electronic address books, calendars, and communication devices; some handhelds can be used as cellular phones to make calls or access the Internet to get news and email. Handhelds have very limited upgradeability. Key attributes are convenience and portability. Pocket PC, Personal Digital Assistant (PDA), and Blackberry are examples of handheld devices.

 The terms "laptop" and "notebook" are often used interchangeably. A notebook will not have a CD-ROM drive built into it and, therefore, notebook computers are much smaller than laptops.

Other Computer Classifications

It is useful to know that there are other types of more powerful computers that can process information much faster and accommodate larger groups of people accessing the machine at the same time.

A *minicomputer* is slightly larger and faster than the PC classification and capable of supporting up to hundreds of users simultaneously—these are very common in company settings.

A *mainframe* is faster than the minicomputer classification and can provide services to hundreds or thousands of users at the same time. Mainframes are frequently used to run multiple programs at the same time.

At the top of the computer power pyramid is the supercomputer. A *supercomputer* is the fastest computer classification and is often used in research and simulation by hospitals, universities, and governments to accomplish a single, specialized task.

Uses of Personal Computers

PCs, being small and powerful, are used in nearly every facet of modern day life. They are designed for individual use and provide a wide range of functions and services applicable to varied environments such as offices, homes, hospitals, schools, and businesses. Personal computers help organizations create and manage data efficiently. PCs can also be used at home for tracking and maintaining income and expense details. Some of the advancements achieved through the use of PCs include shopping on the Internet and touching up digital photos.

Some of the most common tasks a PC can help you with include:

- Budgeting and performing accounting tasks.
- Analyzing numeric information.
- Searching through lists or reports for specific information.
- Scheduling and planning projects.
- Creating illustrations.
- Gaming purposes.
- And, communicating by using electronic mail (email).

ACTIVITY 1-1
Identifying Personal Computers and Their Uses

Scenario:
Your manager has decided to purchase personal computers for the office. You are going to make a list of tasks that you can accomplish once you receive your new personal computer.

1. What do you call the electronic components of a personal computer?

    a) Software

    b) Hardware

    c) Mainframe

    d) Laptop

2. Identify some of the uses of personal computers that you are aware of. (Choose three.)

    a) Create and manage data.

    b) Perform accounting tasks.

    c) Send an electronic mail message.

    d) Deposit cash in ATM.

3. True or False? A personal computer is sometimes referred to as a minicomputer.

    ___ True

    ___ False

Introduction to Personal Computers Using Windows® 7

ACTIVITY 1-2
Identifying Types of Personal Computers

Scenario:
You know a lot about the various types of computers. Your friends John and Laura have come to you and asked you to help them purchase computers.

1. John needs a personal computer that is portable so that he can use it at office and at home, when necessary. He might need it for typical office tasks such as accounting, creating letters and reports, and analyzing numeric information. What will you recommend?

    a) Desktop

    b) Notebook

    c) Handheld

    d) Mainframe

2. Laura needs a personal computer at the office. It needs to be powerful and easy to upgrade because she intends to use it to create and modify graphics. It does not have to be portable. The price is also an issue because she has a budget and she needs to stay within. What will you recommend?

    a) Notebook

    b) Handheld

    c) Desktop

    d) Minicomputer

3. John needs a personal computer that he can carry with him wherever he goes. He does a lot of traveling, so it needs to be small and light enough. What will you recommend?

    a) Supercomputer

    b) Desktop

    c) Mainframe computer

    d) Handheld

TOPIC B
Identify Input Devices

You have identified the different types of personal computers. Now, you are ready to identify the input devices that help you communicate with your computer. In this topic, you will examine input devices.

Assume that you have bought a new car to travel to your office everyday. However, owning the car alone does not get you to your destination. You need to provide it with input such as gasoline. Similarly, to use a PC effectively to create and manage your tasks, you will have to provide some basic input. There are numerous devices that you can use.

Keyboards

A *keyboard* is an input device that is made up of individual keys presented in a standard arrangement of characters representing numerals from 0 through 9, alphabet, and symbols. Apart from entering data, the keyboard can also be used to control the cursor and the dialog between the user and the computer. The different types of keys present on the keyboard are the keys for typing, the numeric keypad, the function keys, and the control keys.

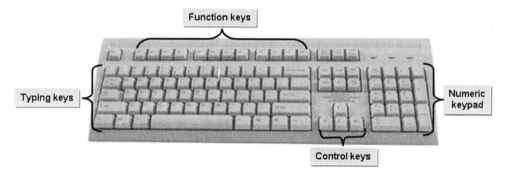

Figure 1-2: A keyboard with the different types of keys.

The Cursor

The *cursor* is a moving pointer that indicates a position. It is also referred to as the insertion point. The insertion point on the screen indicates where the text or graphics will be inserted or erased.

The Mouse

The *mouse* is a small handheld input device used for moving the cursor on the computer screen. The primary functions of the mouse include controlling the motion of the cursor in a graphical user interface and issuing commands to the computer. Usually, a mouse has at least two buttons: a left and a right mouse button. It may have additional buttons or a scroll wheel. The mouse is connected to the computer by a cable, or a tail. Under the mouse is a ball, which senses the movement of the mouse and mirrors the movement on screen.

Figure 1-3: The mouse that is used to control the motion of the cursor in a graphical user interface and issue commands to the computer.

Scanners

A *scanner* is an input device that reads hard copy text, illustrations, or graphs, and translates the information into an electronic form the computer can use. The scanner works by transforming an image to the digital form. It divides the image into a grid of boxes. The resulting *bit map* can be stored in a file, displayed on a screen, and manipulated by a program.

Figure 1-4: A scanner that is used to read and translate information into an electronic form.

USB Devices

A *Universal Serial Bus (USB)* device is a standard, compact removable storage device that can be connected to any personal computer, which has a USB port and USB driver. Some of the popular USB devices include portable flash memory devices, digital cameras, webcams, handheld computers, and optical mice. Once you insert a USB device into a USB port on a personal computer, you can copy or move data between the USB device and the personal computer. The advantage of using a USB device is that you can quickly plug it in and out of a computer without having to reboot the operating system.

Introduction to Personal Computers Using Windows® 7

Figure 1-5: *The flash drive that is used to copy or move data between the USB device and the personal computer.*

Other Input Devices

Apart from the keyboard and the mouse, there are other devices that can be used to enter information into the computer. The following table describes each type of input device.

Input Device	*Description*
Joystick	 A lever that moves in all directions and controls the movement of a pointer or some other display symbol. Joysticks are most commonly used with computer games.
Trackball	 A device that is often used with laptop computers. It works like an upside-down mouse. A trackball requires less desk space than a mouse. Instead of rolling it around the desk, you roll it in place to move the pointer.

Lesson 1: Getting Started with Personal Computers

Input Device	Description
Touchscreen	 A display system that can detect the location of touches within the display area. This allows the display to be used as an input device.

ACTIVITY 1-3
Identifying Input Devices

Scenario:
Your friends Jim and Laura are having trouble identifying the various input components of their computer and their uses. They approach you to help them identify the components.

1. **Jim has purchased a new laptop. Which input device will he use?**

    a) Mouse

    b) Touchscreen

    c) Trackball

    d) Joystick

2. **Laura wants to type a letter. Which device in the computer will help her do her work?**

    a) Monitor

    b) Trackball

    c) Keyboard

    d) Touchscreen

3. **Laura wants to save her family photographs on the computer. Which device will she use to digitalize them first?**

    a) Scanner

    b) Printer

    c) Monitor

    d) Mouse

4. **True or False? Jim is interested in flight stimulator games. He is sure that he can play the game using a touchscreen.**

    ___ True

    ___ False

5. **What are the advantages of using a USB device? (Choose two.)**

   a) You can touch up digital photos.

   b) You can insert the device to read hard copy text and translate the information into an electronic form the computer can use.

   c) You can copy or move data between the USB device and the personal computer.

   d) You can plug and unplug the device without rebooting the operating system.

TOPIC C
Identify Output Devices

You examined the input devices of a computer. Having provided the necessary input to the computer, you now need to view the corresponding output. In this topic, you will examine the various output devices.

PCs work similar to human beings. Just as the human brain processes input information and then communicates the result, the PC also delivers an output to the user. For the computer to communicate with the user, it needs output devices.

Monitors

A *monitor* is a device that enables users to view text and graphical data associated with a computer program. Referred to as the display or computer screen, it displays the computer's open programs, text entered using the keyboard, and cursor movements as indicated by the movements of the mouse.

A monitor is distinguished by its *resolution*. Resolution refers to the sharpness and clarity of images displayed. The thousands of tiny dots on the monitor called *pixels* determine the clarity of the image. The most common type of monitor displays 1024 by 768 pixels, the *SVGA* standard.

Figure 1-6: *The monitor that enables users to view text and graphical data.*

Features of a Monitor

The quality of the monitor is important because a lot of time is spent looking at it. The better the quality of the screen, the longer you can look at it. Based on a few features, monitors may vary.

The following table describes the features of monitors.

Feature	Description
Monitor size	Is measured in inches diagonally across the screen. The majority of computers are sold with a 15" or 17" monitor. They are economical and the size is adequate for most uses.
Anti-glare monitor	Is used to reduce reflections from light sources that make viewing the screen difficult. Some monitors have coated glass to reduce reflections.
Flat or rounded monitor	Is a regular monitor that has a round screen that causes some image distortion. Flat-screen monitors are more expensive, but they cause less image distortion.
Monitor stand	Is used to support the monitor. Some monitors have tilt and swivel stands that make viewing easier.
Controls	Is used to control the functionality of a computer and is usually grouped together, well labeled, and easy to reach.

Computer Cards

Computer cards enable computers to perform certain specific functions that increase the capability of a computer. Some of the computer cards that have become an essential part of a personal computer are video cards, sound cards, and network cards.

Card	Description
Video	A *video card*, sometimes called the graphics card or video adapter is the component that generates images and outputs them to a display unit. The video card interprets information from the computer processor, also called the CPU and sends it to the monitor. It can be built into the circuit board of the computer. When integrated into the circuit board, it uses the computer's temporary memory.
Sound	The *sound card* is the component that facilitates a computer to output audio signals through the attached speakers or the headphones. The sound card usually interprets information from the CPU and converts it into audio signals. Sound cards also allow speech or other sounds to be input and digitized by a computer.

Card	Description
Network	A *network card,* sometimes called the network adapter or network interface card is a component that extends a computer's capabilities to enable it to communicate with other computers and devices on a network. It comprises a circuit board that plugs into both the computer and server, connecting them to the transmission medium, and controls the exchange of data between them.

Printers

A *printer* is a device that is used to transfer a copy of the information that is either stored on your computer or displayed on your screen onto a sheet of paper. Some printers offer special features, such as color and large page formats.

Figure 1-7: A printer that is used to transfer a copy of stored information to paper.

There are three common types of printers. The following table describes each of them.

Printer Type	Description
Laser printers	Laser printers are similar to copy machines. The computer sends the laser printer a computerized copy of the image. It attracts a dry ink called toner, which melts onto the page to leave a permanent, high-quality image.
	Laser printers are expensive; they produce high-quality printouts quietly and quickly. Laser printer speeds are often rated in pages per minute, or ppm.

Printer Type	Description
Inkjet printers	Inkjet printers are less expensive than laser printers, and they produce high-quality printouts quietly; however, they are slow. Inkjet printers are appropriate when you need sharp laser-quality text. However, to print graphics, inkjet printers cannot produce the same quality output as laser printers. Inkjet printers are portable. Inkjet printers are the best option if you want a good resolution color printer.
Dot-matrix printers	Dot-matrix printers are generally the least expensive and the most versatile; however, they are slow and noisy. The print quality is lower than laser or inkjet printers. Dot-matrix printers are the only printers that can handle multi-part forms, such as invoices and carbons. This is because of the impact technology, where the pins actually strike the paper. Dot-matrix printers can use a sheet feeder, a tractor feeder, or both. Sheet feeders work with standard office stationery. Tractor feeders use continuous fan-folded paper, appropriate for lengthy printouts.

Printer Choices

Choosing the right printer will help you achieve the print quality you want at an affordable price. Choosing the right printer involves the following considerations:

- The quality of printing required.
- The speed of printing.
- The size of the printout.
- The type of paper to print on.
- The cost issue (including the expense of consumables).

Printer Costs

Cost per page (CPP) refers to the cost of consumable, or the cost of print supplies that must be periodically replaced. The ink cartridges used in an inkjet printer are consumable and costly. Consumables on the laser printer consist of the toner and drum. The cost of consumables on a color printer is much higher than on a black and white printer.

The Modem

Modem is short for modulator-demodulator. It enables the PC to connect to the Internet and transfer data over telephone lines. Computer information is stored digitally, while telephone lines transmit data in the form of analog waves. A PC's modem converts the data back and forth between these two forms. Modems are often used for inexpensive, low-speed dial-up access to the Internet over ordinary public telephone lines.

Figure 1-8: *The modem that enables a PC to connect to the Internet and transfer data over telephone lines.*

Uses of Modems

The modern modem, being fast and inexpensive, has many uses.

- Online services: With most services, you can send and receive electronic mail. Most services also enable you to receive news, sports, and weather reports; shop and bank at home; make travel plans and reservations; perform research; and take college courses. Online services also provide educational and reference resources and games.

- File transfer: Copying files and programs from another computer to your computer or downloading, and copying a file from your computer to another computer, or uploading is possible.

- Fax services: A fax modem enables you to use your computer to send and receive faxes through a fax machine, or another computer that is equipped with a fax modem.

Data Compression

Computer information can be compressed in size to increase the transmission speed. The compression system lets you reduce the overall number of bits and bytes in a file so that the file can be transmitted faster over slower Internet connections, or take up less space on a disk. Once the file is downloaded, the computer uses a program to restore the file to its original size.

Speakers

Speakers are an output device that provide an audio output when an audio file is played. Speakers are usually equipped with a low-power internal amplifier. They take the electrical signal on a file and translate it back into physical vibrations to create sound waves.

Figure 1-9: Speakers that provide an audio output.

ACTIVITY 1-4
Identifying Output Devices

Scenario:
Your friends Jim and Laura are working with their new computer. They want to be sure that they understand the computer parts and how each part functions.

1. Identify the devices that you feel will most directly aid Jim in his job as a photographer. (Choose two.)

    a) Scanner

    b) Printer

    c) Joystick

    d) Keyboard

2. True or False? The video card in Jim's computer enables him to view images on the monitor.

    __ True

    __ False

3. Laura needs to print inventory lists on a regular basis, but overall quality is not important. Which printer must she use?

    a) The laser printer

    b) The inkjet printer

    c) The dot-matrix printer

    d) The copy machine

4. Jim needs to print reports with high quality text and graphics. Which printers can he use? (Choose two.)

    a) The dot-matrix printer

    b) The laser printer

    c) The inkjet printer

    d) The copy machine

TOPIC D
Identify Storage Devices

You are familiar with the input and output devices of the computer. Another critical need is that of storage devices for permanent storage of data. In this topic, you will identify the different storage devices.

Computer memory is similar to human memory. It can hold only a specific amount of information. Just as people write down information to use it later, a computer stores information on a disk for later use. Also, the information previously saved to a storage device can be retrieved (or read) into computer memory.

Disk Drives

Disk drives are used to permanently store and retrieve information. There are several types of them. In a hard disk drive, the majority of your information is stored even when the PC is turned off. A hard disk is also referred to as a mass storage device rightfully because most hard disks can store a million, if not more, pieces of information. Other common disk drive types include a 3.5 inch floppy-disk drive and CD-ROM or other optical-disk drives. These are called removable storage devices because, in and of themselves, the drives do not store any information. Instead, data is stored on removable media like a 3.5 inch floppy disk or compact disc.

Types of Storage Devices

Storage devices hold data, even when the computer is turned off. The two primary storage technologies are optical and magnetic. The following table describes each type of storage device.

Storage Device Type	Description
Floppy disk	A magnetic storage medium that is composed of a thin, flexible disk encased in a square plastic shell. It stores information on both sides of the disk. Its storage capacity is 1.4 MB. The floppy disk drive, a component of the system unit, stores and retrieves data from a floppy disk.
CD-ROM	A compact disc capable of storing data up to 1 GB. CD-ROMs are stamped by the vendor and cannot be erased and filled with new data. The CD-ROM drive reads the data in the CD-ROM.
DVD-ROM	A read-only compact disc having the capacity to hold 4.7 GB to 17 GB and access rates of 600 KB to 1.3 KB. The DVD-ROM drive can read data from CD-ROMs, CD disks, and video CDs.

Storage Device Type	Description
CD-W	An optical disc used to store digital data. This lets you record your own CDs, but data cannot be overwritten once it is recorded to the disk. The CD-ROM and DVD-ROM can retrieve the data in a CD-W.
CD-RW	A re-recordable disc, which lets you record a CD, then write new data over the already recorded data. The data in the CD-RW is retrieved by CD-ROM but to write to a CD-RW, a CD writer is required.
USB Flash Drive	A compact, removable storage device that can be used to store and transfer information between computers. You can plug the USB flash drive into the USB port of a computer in order to transfer information. Storage capacities typically range from 64 MB to 32 GB. USB flash drives come in many sizes and shapes, and may be sold under names such as a thumb drive, jump drive, or pen drive.

Data Storage

All types of disk storage devices share common elements. On all disks, physical differences in the surface of the disk are used to represent data. On floppy and hard disks, magnetism is used to encode data as a series of 0s and 1s. On CD-ROMs, variations in how the disk surface reflects light are used to encode data.

Care of Disks

Disks, unless cared for and properly handled, may become unusable. The following precautions need to be taken when handling disks.

- Don't touch the surface of the disk.
- Store disks in a disk file box to protect them from dust.
- Store disks in a cool, dry place to avoid exposing them to water, direct sunlight, or heat.
- Keep disks away from magnets, because they can erase data from the disks. This includes paper clip dispensers and some electronic devices, such as telephones, TVs, and speakers.
- Do not send disks through the metal detector at airport security gates. This can affect floppy disks. Request that they be inspected manually.
- Allow the computer to finish writing to a disk before ejecting it.

The Hard Disk

The *hard disk* is a fixed component within the computer that is used to permanently store information needed to boot the computer. It is enclosed within the system unit, and the disk-drive light is on when it is in use. Hard disks generally store large amounts of information. Hard drives come in several sizes, namely 2.5 inch, 3.5 inch, 5.25 inch, and 8 inch. The capacity of a hard disk drive is usually measured in gigabytes. A typical hard drive would have a capacity of 120 GB.

Figure 1-10: The hard disk drive that is used to store information permanently.

ACTIVITY 1-5
Identifying the Storage Devices

Scenario:
Your friend, Jim, has decided to assemble a computer with minimum functionality. He has approached you to help him decide on the minimum requirements of the storage devices.

1. **Jim is a photographer. He needs to copy his work onto a storage medium that has a minimum capacity of 100 MB and distribute his photos to clients. Which device will you recommend to accomplish this?**

    a) Floppy drive

    b) CD-RW drive

    c) DVD drive

    d) Joystick

2. **Which storage device is rewritable and capable of storing a fairly large amount of data?**

    a) CD-ROM

    b) Floppy disk

    c) USB flash drive

    d) CD-W

3. **True or False? The operating system needed to start Jim's computer is stored in the computer hard disk.**

    ___ True

    ___ False

TOPIC E
Set Up the Computer

You are familiar with the input and output devices, and devices for storing information. Now, to start working on your computer you will have to connect the devices. In this topic, you will set up the computer.

Whether in the office or at home, in the twenty-first century, people spend a lot of time working and playing on the computer. Considering all the time spent at a computer, it is important to be aware of how the design and arrangement of the equipment can impact our comfort, health, and productivity.

The Central Processing Unit

The *Central Processing Unit (CPU)* is a tiny electronic chip within the system unit. It is installed on the main circuit board of the computer, the *motherboard*. The CPU is where information is processed within the computer. In terms of calculating power, the CPU is the most important component in a PC. The speed of the CPU is usually measured in *megahertz* or *gigahertz*.

Figure 1-11: The CPU is a chip where information is processed.

Speed of the CPU

A *cycle* is the smallest unit of time recognized by a PC. Each command requires a set number of cycles, so a CPU's speed determines how many commands per second the microprocessor can execute. The higher the value, the better the computer's performance and, generally, the more expensive the chip.

The Front Panel

The system unit or the main box of a computer contains all the key components of the computer including the CPU. The front panel of the system unit contains many buttons and switches.

- Keylock: Locks the keyboard to prevent unauthorized use.
- Power switch: Turns on the system unit.
- Power light: Shows that the computer is on.
- Reset button: Restarts the computer without turning it off.
- Hard-disk light: Indicates when the hard-disk drive is in use.
- CD-ROM light: Indicates when the CD-ROM is in use.

Computer Ports

Definition:

A computer *port* is an outlet on your PC that helps you connect to external hardware. A port enables your computer to send and receive information to and from the peripheral devices you are using. Common ports on PCs include serial, parallel, and Universal Serial Bus (USB). Most newer PC components use either USB or IEEE 1394 ports.

Example:

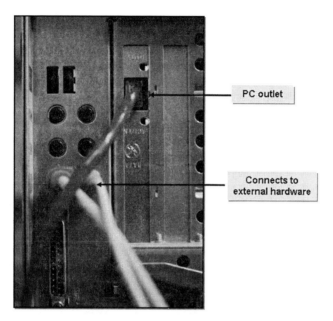

Figure 1-12: The computer port that helps you connect to external hardware.

IEEE 1394 Ports

An IEEE 1394 port is an input or output bus that is gaining popularity in personal computers due to its capability of transferring data at high speeds of up to 400 megabits per second. An IEEE port can connect up to 63 devices, and is capable of transferring data in an uninterrupted manner and at a guaranteed rate.

Hooking It All Up: Cables and Ports

After you know where you want to place everything, you are ready to start connecting the parts with the cables. The cables have cable connectors at each end for attaching your peripherals to the system unit.

Position all equipment so that they are ready to be attached with cables. To attach cables, align them with the port and push in the cable connector. You may need to tighten the cable using the thumbscrews at the end of the connector. Attach the power cord to the system unit and to the monitor. The keyboard has only one cable. Connect the keyboard to the system unit by aligning the pins in the plug with the holes in the socket. Connect the mouse by aligning the mouse port to the system unit. Use the monitor cable to attach the monitor to the monitor port on the system. The printer cable, having a d-shaped connector with 25 pins on one end, goes into the PC's parallel port, sometimes referred to as LPT1 and the other end attaches to the printer.

If you do not see words or pictures, try to match the cables with their ports. Look at the overall shape of the port and see if it has pins or sockets and how many of each.

Physical Location for a Computer

A computer placed in a proper location will ensure a safe place to work.

Guidelines

Follow the guidelines when you set up a computer:

- Location: Choose a place for your computer that is out of the main traffic lane. This will decrease the likelihood of mishaps, such as people banging on the computer or pulling out the plugs.

- Furniture: Choose a sturdy table or desk to place the system. If you have a printer, it is wise to have a separate printer stand. Place the printer in a location where it is easy to load paper. Set the mouse to the right or left of your computer, depending on whether you are left-handed or right-handed.

- Cables and wires: A computer involves a lot of cables and wires, so you have to plan about routing the cables. All the cables and wires should be placed behind the desk where they will not be kicked, tripped over, or pulled. If a modem is included, then the system must be placed near a phone jack.

- Air: Both the system unit and the monitor are electronic devices that need air to cool them. Try to leave three inches of space around both components. The fan inside the power supply, within the system unit, depends upon the air outside the box to circulate the air inside the computer case. This prevents internal components from overheating.

- Lighting: Avoid placing your PC where light will shine on the monitor and cause glare. Lighting, such as a small lamp above the computer and desk, illuminates the paperwork, but not the monitor.

Example:

Georgina purchased a computer and a table to set it on. She placed the table in the corner of the room away from the window. There was adequate lighting and an electrical outlet away from the reach of her children.

Ergonomics

Ergonomics is the study of the problems of people in adjusting to their environment, especially the science that seeks to adapt work and working conditions to suit a worker. Ergonomics aims to make the interaction of humans with machines as smooth as possible, enhancing their performance, reducing error, and increasing user satisfaction through comfort and aesthetics.

Poor posture, lack of proper equipment, and incorrect ergonomic information are the contributing factors to an improper computer setup. People who use computers for a living are prone to a disorder called *Repetitive Strain Injury (RSI)*. The most common repetitive strain injury is called *Carpal Tunnel Syndrome (CTS)*.

RSI and CTS

RSI is a painful condition associated with doing a particular activity repeatedly or for long periods of time. CTS is a painful disorder caused by a buildup of tissue in the nerve channels of the hands and wrists.

Ergonomics of Computing

To avoid ergonomics-related problems:

- The keyboard must be placed at elbow level and the wrists must rest at a proper angle.
- The chair must be adjustable and offer support to the lower back.
- The monitor must be placed at eye level and at a distance of 9 to 12 inches from the face.
- Use an appropriate light source. Light should come from the ceiling or the sides of the monitor.
- The mouse must be held loosely.
- The feet must be placed on the floor or on a stable footrest.
- Use a document holder, preferably in line with the computer screen.
- Take breaks every hour if you need to spend too much time sitting at the computer. Move around to circulate the blood on your hands and fingers.

ACTIVITY 1-6
Identifying an Appropriate Location for the Computer

Scenario:
Your friend John has purchased the latest PC. He now approaches you to help him decide on a proper place to set up the computer and asks for advice on avoiding ergonomic-related problems.

1. **John is searching for a proper place to keep the computer. What will be your suggestion?**

    a) Placing the computer on an existing file cabinet.

    b) Using a wheeled table.

    c) Placing the computer near a window so that there is good ventilation.

    d) Locating the computer in a spare room.

2. **John experiences back pain from arching his neck while viewing the monitor. How could he alleviate the problem? (Choose three.)**

    a) Place the monitor at eye level.

    b) Use a chair which gives support to the lower back.

    c) Rest his head on the chair while working.

    d) Place the monitor at a distance of 9-12 inches.

3. **True or False? Ergonomics is the study of the problems of people in adjusting to their environment.**

    __ True

    __ False

4. **True or False? By keeping a good posture and using proper equipment, John can avoid RSI.**

    __ True

    __ False

TOPIC F
Examine Personal Computer Functionality

You examined the hardware components of a computer and the requirements for setting up the computer. However, computer hardware does not function without software. In this topic, you will examine how hardware and software work in unison to support the basic functions and processes of a personal computer.

Just like the various parts of the human body have their own primary functions, hardware and software within a PC have their own roles and work in coordination to achieve a common goal. When you understand how hardware and software work together, you will have a good grasp of the functions and processes of your personal computer.

Fundamental Computing Processes

From the time the PC is switched on until the time it is switched off, the workings of the PC consist of a cycle of six basic functions.

1. At *startup,* also called *boot,* you turn on the computer, and it performs a number of self-inspections and tests just to make sure everything is working properly.
2. At *data input,* you issue commands or enter information, or *data,* into the software.
3. During *processing,* the computer processes the data by interpreting and executing the data and instructions and then storing them in memory chips.
4. Subsequent to data processing, information processed by the CPU is sent to an output device.
5. If needed, information that will be used later can be transferred to a storage device, such as a disk drive, CD-ROM, or DVD.
6. At shutdown, which is the final step, you will turn off the computer when you are done using your PC.

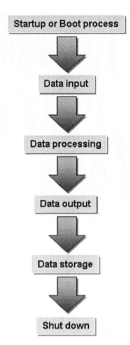

Figure 1-13: A flow chart that displays the six basic computer functions.

The Operating System

Definition:

The *operating system (OS)* is a software program that creates the working environment for the computer, translates between the software and hardware, and helps you manage the hardware and software programs installed on your computer. It is the first program that gets loaded into your computer's memory when the computer is turned on.

Example:

Typical examples of operating systems for IBM-style PCs include Microsoft® Windows® XP, Windows® Vista™, and Windows 7. These operating systems are most often recommended for personal computers. There are other operating systems from other vendors that you can use on personal computers, including Apple's Mac® OS X and various versions of Unix and Linux.

Figure 1-14: The Welcome screen of the Windows 7 operating system that gets loaded into your computer's memory when the computer is turned on.

Memory

Memory is the power dependent area within the computer that stores information. There are several types of computer memory. The term most commonly refers to a set of microchips within the computer, called *random access memory (RAM)*. RAM temporarily stores information to be accessed quickly by the CPU while the PC is running. When the PC is turned off, the information temporarily stored in RAM is emptied. Generally speaking, the more memory a PC has, the greater is its performance and capabilities.

Another type of memory is called *read-only memory (ROM)*. ROM has prerecorded data and it retains its information even when the PC is switched off. ROM stores critical data used when the computer is starting.

Figure 1-15: The computer memory within the computer that stores information.

Memory Measurement Units

Temporary memory, RAM, is measured in small groups of data called bytes. The *byte* is the fundamental unit of measure for computer data. One typed character is about one byte. Each byte consists of eight *bits,* which are individual 1s and 0s. On a computer, bits are stored as tiny electrical impulses that act as an on or off signal—to represent the numbers 1 and 0, respectively. By using a combination of bits, the smallest unit of information on a computer system, you can represent any character or number.

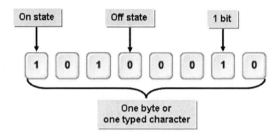

Figure 1-16: *The memory measurement units that are measured in small groups of data called bytes.*

Each byte is very tiny, so other terms are often used to measure larger amounts of memory.

Memory Unit	Description
Byte	One character (a letter, number, space, or punctuation mark). A byte consists of eight bits.
Kilobyte (K)	1,024 bytes or 8,192 bits constitute one kilobyte.
Megabyte (MB, Meg, or M)	1,048,576 bytes or 1,024 kilobytes constitute one megabyte.
Gigabyte (GB)	1,073,741,824 bytes or 1,024 MB constitute one gigabyte.

The Boot Process

To work on your computer, you need to start the operating system. Your computer has a small program that remains in memory, even when the power is turned off. When you start the PC, this program runs and begins what is known as the *boot process,* loading the operating system from the hard drive to memory. The boot process also checks for the functionality of the devices connected to your personal computer.

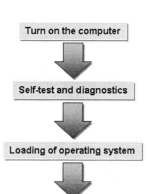

Figure 1-17: The flow chart explaining the boot process that loads the operating system into memory.

The boot process consists of four different stages:

1. First, the user turns on the computer by pressing the power button that is located on the front of the system unit's case.
2. Then, the computer performs a series of self-tests and diagnostics.
3. Subsequently, the computer loads the operating system from the hard drive.
4. Finally, the operating system loads other software that the user specifies to run at startup.

ACTIVITY 1-7
Examining the Personal Computer Functionality

Scenario:
Being a photographer, Jim wants to load the latest software related to his job. He also needs a lot of space on the computer to store the photographs of his clients. Having acquired a new computer recently, he asks for your help.

1. Jim has been advised to restart his computer whenever a new application program is installed on his computer. What is the first thing that happens when Jim restarts the computer?

    a) The computer loads other basic software.

    b) The computer performs a series of self-tests and diagnostics.

    c) The computer loads the operating system.

    d) The computer shuts down automatically.

2. Where does the computer store the new software that Jim has loaded?

    a) In the hard drive

    b) In the RAM

    c) In the ROM

    d) In computer memory

3. True or False? The critical data required for booting a computer is stored in the ROM.

    __ True

    __ False

4. True or False? Jim's computer has 40 GB memory when compared to his colleague's computer memory which is 20 GB. The performance and capabilities of Jim's computer will be better than his colleague's computer.

    __ True

    __ False

Lesson 1 Follow-up

In this lesson, you examined the fundamental concepts of personal computers. Having familiarized yourself with the basics of personal computers, you will now be able to work with them more effectively.

1. **For what purposes do you or your organization use personal computers?**

2. **Discuss the various advancements that you have witnessed in the use of computer technology.**

2 Exploring Windows 7 Operating System

Lesson Time: 1 hour(s), 5 minutes

Lesson Objectives:

In this lesson, you will explore the Windows 7 operating system after logging on to it using the personal computer.

You will:

- Log on to Windows 7 using a user account to access computer programs and functions.
- Explore the desktop to identify its components so that you can quickly access tools and programs.
- Work with windows using the desktop menu options to resize, reposition, and compare two open windows.
- Search for information using the Windows Help and Support feature to get additional information on Windows 7 features.
- Turn off a personal computer using the log off options to log out of the computer.

Introduction

You are familiar with the basics of a personal computer. To start using your computer, you need to have a working knowledge of the operating system that forms the core element of your personal computer. In this lesson, you will explore Microsoft® Windows® 7.

Before starting to work with any software, it is essential that you familiarize yourself with the tools that are available, where they are located, how they can be used, and how you can modify them to suit your needs. This enables you to work with the software effectively and realize its maximum potential. Exploring the Windows 7 environment enables you to build the skills needed to perform more complex tasks.

Introduction to Personal Computers Using Windows® 7

TOPIC A
Log On to Windows 7 Operating System

In order to start using your computer, you need to have a working knowledge of the operating system that forms the core element of your personal computer. To get familiar with the Windows 7 user interface, you need to start exploring the working environment. In this topic, you will log on to Windows 7.

The purpose of a safe is to keep valuable items secure. To open a safe, you need to use the correct combination. The same is true with Windows 7. It allows many people to use the same computer. To keep the information on your computer secure, Windows 7 requires you to log on. This prevents unauthorized users from accessing your computer, keeping its contents safe.

Typing Keys

The typing keys are the most often used keys on the keyboard. These keys are marked with the letters of the alphabet, the numerals from 0 through 9, and additional special operational keys. When a key is held down, it will automatically begin to repeat.

Operational Keys

The operational keys on the keyboard have special functions to perform.

Key	*Function*
Shift	These keys have no effect by themselves. They are used to shift the keyboard to upper-case letters and special characters, such as the dollar sign.
Caps Lock	When **Caps Lock** is turned on, characters you type appear as capital letters. The **Caps Lock** indicator lights when this switch is turned on. The **Caps Lock** key has no effect on numbers or punctuation marks.
Enter	This key marks the end of a line.
Spacebar	This key creates a space.
Tab	This key indents to the next tab stop.
Backspace	This key erases the character to the left of the insertion point. Use it to make corrections as you type.

The Numeric Keypad

The set of keys on the right of the keyboard is called the *numeric keypad,* which works like a calculator or adding machine. It features digits from 0 to 9 and arithmetic operators such as addition, subtraction, multiplication, and division. It provides a quick and convenient way to enter long lists of numbers. In the upper-left corner of the numeric keypad is a key labeled **Num Lock.** When **Num Lock** is turned on, which is indicated by a glowing light either above the key or a little away from it, you can use the numeric keypad to type numbers. When **Num Lock** is turned off, you use the numeric keypad to move around on screen.

Figure 2-1: The numeric keypad present on the right side of the keyboard.

Function Keys

The *function keys* are marked **F1, F2, F3,** and so on. The "F" on these keys stands for "function." The way the function keys work depends on the program you are running. Often they are designated as shortcuts to common tasks. Although designers of computer programs can designate the use of each function key, some uses have become almost standard. For example, in most programs, you can press **F1** to get help.

Figure 2-2: The twelve function keys present at the top-half of the keyboard.

Control Keys

The *control keys* provide cursor and screen control. The control keys are the two sets of keys placed between the typing keys and the numeric keypad. The bottom set is arranged in an inverted T formation and marked with an arrow that shows which way the insertion point moves when you press the key.

Figure 2-3: The control keys on the keyboard.

The following table describes the functions of the control keys.

Key	Use
Insert	Switches between Insert and Overtype modes. The Insert mode typically enables you to insert or add letters between existing characters. The Overtype mode replaces characters as you type.
Delete	Deletes the character to the right of the insertion point.
Home	Moves to the beginning of a line.
End	Moves to the end of a line.
Page Up	Moves one page up toward the beginning of the document.
Page Down	Moves one page down toward the end of the document.

The Ctrl and Alt Keys

The **Ctrl** and **Alt** keys do nothing when pressed alone. These keys are used in combination with other keys such as a letter key or a function key to give commands to programs and do useful functions.

Rebooting

There is a special key combination that takes advantage of the **Ctrl** and **Alt** keys. To restart a computer, the **Ctrl+Alt+Del** keys are pressed simultaneously. This is called a *warm boot*. A warm boot is faster than a *cold boot* because the operating system does not check all of its hardware and memory. Turning off the power and then turning the machine back on is called a cold boot.

Other Computer Keys

There are other computer keys, each of which has a very specific function.

Key	Use
Print Screen	Sends the screen image to the printer.
Scroll Lock	Stops the screen from scrolling.
Pause	Temporarily halts the action of the program being run.
Esc	Usually cancels a command. In many programs, **Esc** returns you to the previous menu screen or closes a menu.

Mouse Controls

While working on a computer, you will have to use the mouse, the flat bottom of which has a little ball. When you move the mouse on a flat clean surface, the ball rolls and comes in contact with a set of rollers inside the mouse's casing. The rollers send signals to the CPU, which interprets them and moves a small icon, called the mouse pointer on the display screen. An optical or a digital mouse does not have a little ball or rollers. It uses digital signals to move the mouse pointer. However, using an optical mouse is essentially the same as using a standard mouse.

Depending upon what the mouse pointer is near, the icon may assume a variety of shapes such as a left-pointing arrow, a right-pointing arrow, an index finger, or an I-beam. When the system is busy processing instructions and cannot respond to any input, the icon changes to an hourglass. You should place your mouse on a clean, flat surface such as a small rubber or plastic mat, called a mouse pad to enable the mouse to be more responsive to your hand's movements.

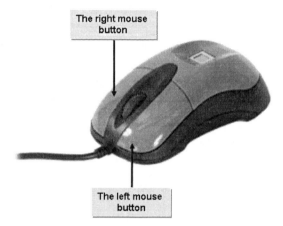

Figure 2-4: The buttons on the mouse.

Removing the Mouse Ball

It is a good idea to remove and clean the mouse ball occasionally because dust gathers on the roller bar inside the mouse. You might detect when it is time to clean it if, after extended use, the mouse pointer does not move smoothly.

Mouse Actions

A standard PC mouse has two buttons. By default, the left button is primary and the right is secondary. There are five general actions that you can perform with the mouse to accomplish a wide variety of tasks.

The following table describes different mouse actions.

Action	Description
Point/Hover/Rollover	Position the mouse pointer over an item.
Click	Hold the mouse steady, and then press and release the left (primary) mouse button. This places the mouse pointer in a desired location, selects an object, or starts a command.

Action	Description
Double-click	Press and release the left (primary) mouse button twice in rapid succession. This selects or opens an object or starts a command.
Right-click	Hold the mouse still and then press and release the right (secondary) mouse button. This displays a shortcut menu to perform many common actions.
Drag	Hold down the left (primary) mouse button while moving the mouse. This moves a selected object or selects content on the screen.

Mouse Control Tips

It is important to keep your hand steady when clicking. Be quick with the double-click. Two single clicks do not necessarily make a double-click. If you click twice slowly, you will select an item twice.

Customizing Mouse Settings

You can customize the way you use your mouse. For example, you might want to slow down the speed of a double-click, or switch the functions of the left and right mouse buttons. The **Control Panel** is a Windows application that enables you to change some of your computer system's hardware and software options.

User Accounts

Definition:

A *user account* is an information profile that uniquely identifies a user on a computer. Every user account on a computer needs to have a unique *user name* and *password*. Users can set their own passwords. Different users on the same computer may have different *rights* and *permissions* that enable them to access resources and perform specific tasks such as printing or installing new applications.

Example:

Assume that two people, John and Laura, work on two different shifts and use the same computer. John's work involves preparation of documents, while Laura is involved in Internet research. Both John and Laura will have separate user names and passwords to access the computer. However, they may have different permissions. For instance, since John's work involves documentation, he may have permissions to use printer resources within the organization, while Laura, who is involved in Internet research, may have permissions to download and store large amounts of data on the computer.

Protecting Passwords

As you type your user account's password, each character is displayed as a black circle to prevent someone looking over your shoulder from seeing your password.

User Account Information

The following table provides some more information about the important characteristics of user accounts.

User Account Characteristic	Description
User name	A unique name identifying a user on a computer.
Password	A case-sensitive string of alphanumeric characters that must be typed before a user can access a computer. A password acts as a key to log in to your computer. A strong password is a combination of both uppercase and lowercase letters, numbers, and special characters.
Permissions and rights	A set of rules that determine what things a user is allowed to do on a computer and what resources the user can access; by limiting a user's permissions and rights, you can keep the person from opening files, installing unwanted software, or changing certain computer settings.

The Welcome Screen

The *Windows 7 Welcome screen* that is displayed when you switch on the computer allows you to access programs and applications on your system. It lists all the user accounts on the computer and lets you choose a user account to log on. The **Welcome** screen displays the **Ease of access** button, the **Shut down** button, and the **Shut down options** menu.

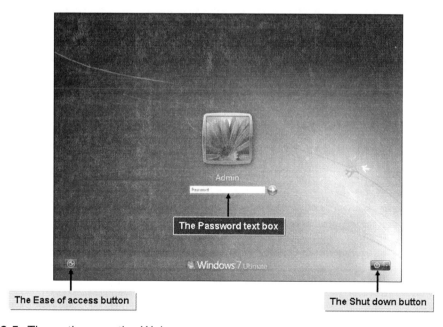

Figure 2-5: The options on the Welcome screen.

The Ease of Access Button

The *Ease of access button,* located at the bottom-left corner of the Windows 7 **Welcome** screen, provides the accessibility options that help users with disabilities to navigate easily within the operating system. When you click this button, the **Ease of Access** dialog box opens, and the audio automatically reads the options available for users to enable features such as **Narrator, Magnifier, High Contrast, On-Screen Keyboard, Sticky Keys,** and **Filter Keys.**

Audio Settings

Ensure that the required audio settings are configured for the narration feature to work. You must have an inbuilt sound card and the necessary audio drivers installed on your system. If your system does not have internal speakers, you can connect to an external speaker or headphones to hear the narration.

Ease of Access Options

The following table lists the **Ease of Access** options.

Option	Description
Hear text on screen read aloud (Narrator)	Reads all the highlighted screen elements.
Make items on the screen larger (Magnifier)	Magnifies the highlighted section on the screen.
See more contrast in colors (High Contrast)	Displays the screen in High Contrast mode.
Type without the keyboard (On-Screen Keyboard)	Enables the on-screen keyboard so that you can click it to type text using the mouse instead of the regular physical keyboard.
Press keyboard shortcuts one key at a time (Sticky Keys)	Enables the sticky keys so that you can press one key instead of a combination of several keys at once.
If I press keys repeatedly, ignore extra presses (Filter Keys)	Enables the filter keys to avoid unintended successive strokes of a specific key on the keyboard.

The Shut Down Options Menu

The *Shut down options menu,* located at the bottom-right corner of the **Welcome** screen, enables you to quickly apply a power setting without the need to log on to your computer. This menu provides you with different power options such as **Restart, Sleep,** and **Shut down.**

How to Log On to Windows 7

Procedure Reference: Configure the Ease of Access Options

To configure the **Ease of Access** options:

1. Switch on the computer.
2. On the **Welcome** screen, at the bottom-left corner, click the **Ease of access** button to access the **Ease of Access** dialog box.
3. In the **Ease of Access** dialog box, configure the available options.
4. Click **OK** to save the changes.

Procedure Reference: Log On to Windows 7

To log on to Windows 7:

1. Switch on the computer.
2. On the Windows 7 **Welcome** screen, select the desired user account.
3. In the **Password** text box, type the password and then press **Enter,** or click the right arrow button to log on.

Procedure Reference: Move the Mouse

To move the mouse:

1. Verify that the system is switched on and you are logged on to the user interface.
2. If necessary, ensure the mouse is placed on a mouse pad.
3. Hold the mouse properly.
    a. Lay your hand loosely on top of the mouse.
    b. Place your index finger on the left mouse button, your middle finger on the right mouse button, your thumb on the corresponding side of the mouse, and the ring and little fingers on the other side.
    c. Ensure that your palm is resting comfortably on the back of the mouse.
4. Move the mouse in the required direction to make the mouse pointer move in the corresponding direction on the desktop.

Repositioning the Mouse

If you run out of room when moving the mouse on the mouse pad, just pick up the mouse and reposition it somewhere else on the pad. Picking up the mouse does not move the mouse pointer, but it does give you the opportunity to reposition the mouse so that you have more room to move it.

Introduction to Personal Computers Using Windows® 7

ACTIVITY 2-1
Logging On to Windows 7

Before You Begin:
Switch on your computer.

Scenario:
A personal computer with Windows 7 as the operating system is provided to you by your company. You want to explore the desktop and other components of Windows 7. Before you start working with the new operating system, you like to explore the different logon options available and then log on to the system using the user name and password.

What You Do	How You Do It
1. Explore the **Welcome** screen.	a. On the **Welcome** screen, at the bottom-left corner, click the **Ease of access** button.
	b. In the **Ease of Access** dialog box, observe the available setting options.
	c. Click **Cancel** to close the dialog box.
	d. At the bottom-right corner of the **Welcome** screen, click the **Shut down options** button to display the menu.
	e. Click outside the **Shut down options** menu to close it.
2. Log on to Windows 7.	a. In the **Password** text box, click and type *p@ssw0rd*
	b. Press **Enter** to log on to the system and display the desktop.

Introduction to Personal Computers Using Windows® 7

ACTIVITY 2-2
Using the Mouse

Before You Begin:
The Windows 7 desktop is displayed.

Scenario:
You have now logged on to Windows 7. To get familiar with the PC mouse functionality, you decide to perform a few basic operations using the mouse.

What You Do	How You Do It
1. Select items with the mouse.	a. On the taskbar, hover the mouse pointer over the button located at the extreme left to view the pop-up description.
	b. Hover the mouse pointer over the **Windows Explorer** icon, which is the third icon from the left, to view its description, and then click the icon to launch Windows Explorer.
	c. In the right pane, double-click **Videos** to open the **Videos** folder.
	d. In the left pane, hover the mouse pointer over a link. Observe that the mouse pointer changes to a hand cursor.
	e. Click the **Libraries** link to return to the **Libraries** folder.
	f. Hover the mouse pointer over the **Close** button and click to close Windows Explorer.
2. Drag an item with the mouse.	a. Click the **Recycle Bin** icon to select it.
	b. Hold down the left mouse button and drag the **Recycle Bin** icon to the middle of the screen.
	c. Click and drag the **Recycle Bin** icon back to its original position.
	d. Click an empty area of the desktop to deselect the **Recycle Bin** icon.

3. Display the **Recycle Bin** window using the mouse action.

   a. On the desktop, place the mouse pointer over the **Recycle Bin** icon and right-click the icon.

   b. From the shortcut menu that is displayed, choose **Open.**

   c. Observe that the **Recycle Bin** window is opened.

   d. Click the **Close** button at the top-right corner of the dialog box to close the **Recycle Bin** window.

DISCOVERY ACTIVITY 2-3

Examining the Welcome Screen

Scenario:
You need to start working with the new Windows 7 operating system. Before you begin to work in the actual environment, you decide to test your knowledge of the various logon options that Windows 7 offers and the different mouse actions that can be used while exploring and working with the environment.

1. **Which elements are displayed on the Windows 7 Welcome screen?**

    a) The Shut down options menu

    b) The recently used programs

    c) The user logon options

    d) The Ease of access button

    e) The Start button

2. **Which option allows you to change the accessibility settings before logging on to your computer?**

    a) The Switch User option

    b) The Shut down options menu

    c) The Ease of Access option

    d) The Logon text box

3. **What will be the appropriate mouse action to display a shortcut menu?**

    a) Click

    b) Right-click

    c) Double-click

    d) Drag

TOPIC B
Explore the Desktop

You have now logged on to Windows 7. Once you are logged on, all your activities will be based on the Windows 7 desktop. In this topic, you will explore the Windows 7 desktop.

The desktop is the main interface for you to access tools and programs that are used on a daily basis. Before you can use any of these tools and programs, you need to know what the desktop really is and the options it provides. Once you gain this knowledge, you will be able to accomplish a number of tasks quickly and easily.

The Desktop

The *desktop* is the main screen of Windows 7. It is the work area where windows, icons, and menus appear. From your desktop, you can perform file-management tasks using the items on it and run software applications. You can also customize the appearance of the desktop to suit your preferences.

The Taskbar

The *taskbar* is a rectangular bar located at the bottom of the desktop. The majority of your interaction with the operating system will involve the taskbar in some capacity. By default, it contains the **Start** button, the **Internet Explorer, Windows Explorer,** and **Windows Media Player** icons, the notification area, and the **Show Desktop** button. However, you can pin other programs or applications to the taskbar.

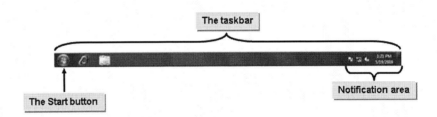

Figure 2-6: The components of the taskbar.

The Start Menu

The *Start menu* is a list of commands that allow you to start programs, open recently used files, search for files and programs, adjust computer settings, and perform other tasks. The left pane of the menu displays the list of frequently used programs. The right pane provides links to the commonly used files and programs such as **Documents, Pictures, Music, Computer,** and **Control Panel.** You can turn off the computer by clicking the **Shut down** button at the bottom of the right pane or hover the mouse pointer over the right pointing arrow next to the **Shut down** button to apply other shut down options. You can pin items to the **Start** menu by right-clicking the item and choosing the **Pin to Start Menu** option. The **Start** menu also displays a context menu when you right-click a menu item.

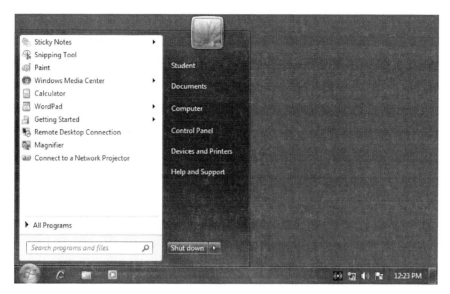

Figure 2-7: The Start menu and its components.

The Notification Area

The *notification area,* displayed at the bottom-right corner of the taskbar, displays system related notifications and provides links to system settings. This area is redesigned to include only the standard status icons such as **Volume, Clock, Network,** and **Action Center.** When you install an application, the application icon is automatically displayed in the notification area. However, you can choose to show or hide such icons and notifications, or show notifications only. When you click the triangle to the left of the notification area, it displays the hidden icons in a window above the taskbar. You can customize the settings and also drag items from a window to the notification area.

Submenus

A *submenu* is a list of options that branches out from a main menu item. A submenu can be easily identified by a right-pointing arrow head positioned on the main menu. A submenu usually consists of options that help you perform tasks related to a broad action item.

Objects

Objects are basic components in Windows 7, represented by small pictures called icons. Files, folders, disk drives, and shortcuts are some of the common objects that you will work with to accomplish your computing tasks.

Types of Objects

The following table lists the three main types of objects.

Object Type	Description
File	A collection of data that is stored under a single name. Your computer uses many types of files. Two of these types include data and program.
	Data files are the documents you create and save. For example, data can be the text of a letter, numbers in a spreadsheet, or a graphical image. Everything you store on your computer, such as letters, spreadsheets, and databases that you create are stored as files.
	Program files execute or start a program. For example, when you install software, you are installing program files.
Container	An object that holds other objects so that you can organize them. Containers come in different forms. For example, a container can be a folder or a disk drive.
	Each container allows you to store files as well as other containers. The desktop includes one container, the Recycle Bin.
Shortcut	A link that points to another file or container object. You can create multiple shortcuts to the same object so that it is easily accessible from multiple locations.
	Shortcut icons look similar to the objects they lead to, except that they have a small arrow in their lower-left corner to indicate that they are shortcuts. Opening a shortcut opens the object that the shortcut points to.

Object Attributes

Object attributes are the characteristic properties that are unique to each object. When you right-click an object and choose the **Properties** option, the **Properties** dialog box of that object is displayed. The dialog box will have one or several property sheets that display the properties of the object. Each property sheet looks like a tabbed page.

How to Explore the Desktop

Procedure Reference: Explore the Desktop

To explore the desktop:

1. Click the **Start** button to display the **Start** menu.
2. View the different options available in the left pane that lists the frequently used programs.
3. Click outside the **Start** menu to close it.
4. On the desktop, right-click the **Recycle Bin** icon and choose **Properties** to view its properties.
5. In the **Recycle Bin Properties** dialog box, click **OK** to close the dialog box.

Introduction to Personal Computers Using Windows® 7

ACTIVITY 2-4
Exploring the Desktop Elements

Before You Begin:
The Windows 7 desktop is displayed with no open programs.

Scenario:
Before you begin to interact with the working environment, you decide to explore the desktop so that you can quickly access the options and programs, whenever you need to work on them.

What You Do	How You Do It
1. Explore the **Start** menu.	a. Click the **Start** button to display the **Start** menu.
	b. On the **Start** menu, in the frequently accessed programs list, hover the mouse pointer over the **Getting Started** item.
	c. Observe that a submenu is displayed with a list of additional items.
	d. Click the **Start** button again to close the **Start** menu.
2. View the properties of the **Recycle Bin**.	a. On the desktop, hover the mouse pointer on the **Recycle Bin** icon to view its pop-up description.
	b. On the desktop, right-click the **Recycle Bin** icon and choose **Properties** to view its properties.
	c. In the **Recycle Bin Properties** dialog box, view the properties and click **OK** to close the dialog box.

DISCOVERY ACTIVITY 2-5

Identifying Desktop Elements

Scenario:
You have just explored the desktop in Windows 7. You now decide to test yourself to find if you can identify the various desktop elements.

1. Which among the following is a container object?

    a) Shortcut to C disk drive

    b) A word document file

    c) The C disk drive

    d) A pop-up description of a program

2. Which elements are found on the Start menu?

    a) The Shut down options

    b) The link to Control Panel

    c) The Show Desktop option

    d) A list of recently used files

    e) Frequently accessed programs

TOPIC C
Work with Windows

You explored the desktop. Once you launch a program from the desktop or any other location, it becomes a window so that you can begin using it. In this topic, you will work with open windows.

Windows are the most fundamental items in the Windows 7 operating system. In fact, whenever you choose an option from the **Start** menu, a window will be opened on your desktop, providing you with a way to interact with that program. Sometimes, you may have to work with multiple programs simultaneously. Controlling the position of a window or resizing it becomes crucial when you have to switch between or work with multiple windows.

Window Components

All windows in the Windows 7 operating system have a set of common components and controls that are used to open and edit files in different programs.

The following table describes the common window components.

Component	Location and Description
The *title bar*	Displays the program's name and the name of the file currently opened. It also has three control buttons, *Minimize, Maximize/Restore,* and *Close*.
The *ribbon/menu bar*	Contains several tabs or menus, that in turn, display their commands.
The *status bar*	Provides additional information about the buttons, commands, and processes in the window.

The Control Buttons

Windows contain control buttons that vary depending upon the window state. These buttons are described in the following table.

Control Button	Description
The **Minimize** button	This button is displayed as an underscore character (_) on the title bar. You can click this button to reduce a window to a button on the taskbar. You can keep the window minimized on the taskbar until you are ready to use it again. Clicking the minimized window on the taskbar will restore it to the same state as it was before it was minimized.

Control Button	Description
The **Maximize/Restore** button	The **Maximize** button appears as a square on the title bar, to the right of the **Minimize** button. When you open a window on the desktop, it does not necessarily fill the screen. Clicking the **Maximize** control button makes the window expand to the size of the desktop.
	After a window has been maximized, the **Maximize** button is replaced by a **Restore Down** control button. Click **Restore Down** to return a window to its previous size. The **Restore Down** button appears as two overlapping squares on the title bar.
	You can also change the window size by dragging the border from any side in both restored down and maximized states.
The **Close** button	This button is displayed as an X on the title bar to the right of either the **Maximize** or **Restore Down** button. To close a window, click the **Close** button.

The Active Window

A window must be active to enable you to work with it. When several windows are open, they can overlap, but the active window will be on top. The title bar of the active window will have a different color or shade to distinguish it from the title bar of an inactive window. To make a different window active, click either the window or its corresponding icon on the taskbar.

Title Bar Colors

The title bar of an active window will be of a different shade than the title bar of inactive windows, when the default Windows 7 basic theme is applied. However, when you change the theme and desktop background to an Aero themes-based background, all the title bars will be of the same transparent color.

The Taskbar's Shortcut Menu

You can right-click the taskbar to display a shortcut menu which provides you with options to add toolbars, arrange open windows on the desktop, display the task manager, lock the taskbar, and modify the properties of the taskbar.

Arrange Options on the Taskbar

The following tables lists the arrangement options provided in the taskbar's shortcut menu along with the description.

Option	Description
Cascade windows	Resizes and layers the open windows in a fanned out manner so that each title bar is accessible.

Option	Description
Show windows stacked	Resizes and displays the open windows top to bottom on the desktop.
Show windows side by side	Resizes and displays the open windows side by side on the desktop.
Show the desktop	Minimizes all the open windows and displays the desktop.

Aero Effects

Aero effects provide a rich visual experience with a glossy and transparent user interface, and dynamic visual and animation effects such as glossy window borders, live preview of taskbar icons, and a 3D view of open windows. You can choose a color scheme from one of the pre-defined color schemes, or you can create a custom color scheme using the color mixer. Each color has a default transparency level that can be changed for both predefined and custom color schemes.

The Aero Peek Feature

Using the *Aero Peek feature*, you can display the desktop among a lot of open windows by hovering the mouse pointer over the **Show desktop** button. The open windows will then become transparent, enabling you to view the desktop. However, when you click the **Show desktop** button, the desktop will be fully displayed and you can click the button again to display the active window.

The Snap Feature

The *Snap feature* simplifies the resizing of open windows. To use this feature, you need to click the title bar of the window, drag it to the left or right of the screen, and release the mouse button to arrange two windows to the left and right halves of the screen. You can also drag the window to the top of the screen and release the mouse button to maximize it.

The Shake Feature

The *Shake feature* allows you to keep the active window visible on screen, while minimizing the rest of the open windows. You can use this feature by clicking the title bar of the window you want to keep open and then shaking the window back and forth to minimize other open windows.

Jump Lists

A *jump list* is a list of menu options related to a program or application that is displayed when you right-click a taskbar icon. A jump list is contextual and displays items relevant to a particular application. The common jump list sections include **Pinned, Frequent,** and **Tasks.** You can pin an item to the jump list by clicking the pin icon next to the display name, or right-clicking the list item and choosing **Pin to this list.** You can also remove an item from the jump list.

Figure 2-8: The jump list displaying Internet Explorer options.

How to Work with Windows

Procedure Reference: Start a Program

To start a program:

1. If necessary, log on to the system and ensure that the desktop is displayed.
2. Start the program.
    - Launch a program from the **Start** menu or one of its submenus.
        a. Click the **Start** button.
        b. To open the file or program, click it or right-click it and choose **Open.**
    - Launch a program from a desktop shortcut.
        a. Place the mouse pointer over the shortcut icon.
        b. Double-click to open the file or program.

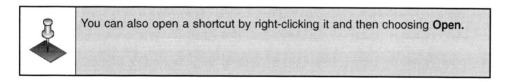

Procedure Reference: Minimize a Window

To minimize a window:

1. If necessary, activate the window.
2. Click the **Minimize** button on the title bar.

Procedure Reference: Minimize All Open Windows Except the Active Window

To minimize all open windows except the active window:

1. If necessary, activate the window.
2. Click on the title bar of the window and shake the window to and fro to minimize the open windows.

Procedure Reference: Maximize a Window

To maximize a window:

1. If necessary, activate the window.
2. Select an Aero theme of your choice.
3. Maximize the window.
   - Click the **Maximize** button to maximize the window, using the title bar.
   - Or, click the title bar of the window, drag it to the top of the screen, and release the mouse pointer.

Procedure Reference: Restore a Window

To restore a window:

1. Locate the necessary window that you want to restore.
2. Restore the window to the previous size.
   - Click the **Restore** button to restore the window, using the title bar.
   - Click on the title bar of the window, drag it away from top of the screen, and release the mouse pointer.

Procedure Reference: Close a Window

To close a window:

1. If necessary, activate the window.
2. Close the window.
   - Click the **Close** button to close the window, using the title bar.
   - Or, close the window by pressing **Alt+F4.**

Procedure Reference: Arrange Windows

To arrange windows:

1. Ensure that you have a minimum of two windows minimized onto your taskbar.
2. Arrange windows.
   - Arrange the windows using the Aero Snap feature.
     1. Click the title bar of the window.
     2. Drag the title bar to the left or right of the screen and release the mouse button to arrange the windows side by side.
   - Right-click the taskbar and choose an option to arrange your open windows.
     - Choose **Cascade windows** to arrange the open windows in a cascading manner.
     - Choose **Show windows stacked** to arrange the windows horizontally and display them from top to bottom.

- Choose **Show windows side by side** to arrange the windows vertically and display them side by side.

Other Controls Used for Handling Windows

You can also right-click the program's taskbar button and choose the desired control option or click the window's **Control** menu icon and choose any control option.

Procedure Reference: Display the Desktop When Multiple Windows Are Opened

To display the desktop when multiple windows are opened:

1. Open the applications you want to work with and keep them maximized.
2. At the far-right corner of the taskbar, click the **Show desktop** button to minimize the open applications.

Procedure Reference: Pin an Item to the Jump List on the Taskbar

To pin an item to the jump list on the taskbar:

1. Ensure that the taskbar icons display jump lists.
2. View a jump list.
   - Right-click the taskbar icon.
   - Or, click the taskbar icon and slide the mouse forward.
3. Pin an item to the jump list.
   - Click the pin icon to the right of the jump list item.
   - Or, right-click the jump list item and choose **Pin to this list.**
4. Observe that the item moves to a new **Pinned** section within the list.

Introduction to Personal Computers Using Windows® 7

ACTIVITY 2-6
Working with Windows

Before You Begin:
The Windows 7 desktop is displayed with no open programs.

Scenario:
Your job requires you to multitask, and therefore, you have several windows open on your system. Windows 7 has made it easy to work with multiple windows. You will use the various options to handle multiple windows.

What You Do	How You Do It
1. Open multiple program windows.	a. On the taskbar, click the **Internet Explorer** icon to display the **Internet Explorer** window.
	b. Choose **Start→Computer**.
2. Manipulate the open windows.	a. Click the title bar of the **Computer** window, drag it to the top of the screen, and release the mouse pointer.
	b. Observe that the window is now maximized for better viewing.
	c. Click the title bar of the **Computer** window, drag it away from the top of the screen, and release the mouse pointer.
	d. Observe that the window is now restored to its previous size.
3. Arrange the windows.	a. Click the title bar of the **Computer** window, drag it to the mid-left of the screen, and release the mouse pointer.
	b. Similarly, click the title bar of the **Internet Explorer** window and drag the window toward the extreme right of the screen, and release the mouse pointer.
	c. Right-click the taskbar and choose **Cascade windows**.
	d. On the title bar of the **Internet Explorer** window, click the **Maximize** button.

4. Display the desktop.

   a. On the taskbar, click the **Show desktop** button to display the desktop.

   b. Click the **Show desktop** button again to display the **Blank Page - Windows Internet Explorer** window.

5. Close all windows.

   a. In the **Blank Page - Windows Internet Explorer** window, on the title bar, click the **Close** button to close the window.

   b. Similarly, close the **Computer** window.

DISCOVERY ACTIVITY 2-7
Examining the Enhanced Features Related to Windows

Scenario:
You have heard much about the new functions that can be performed with open windows in Windows 7. You decide to try them out for yourself.

1. **Which window component displays additional information about the buttons, commands, and processes in the window?**

    a) The menu bar

    b) The toolbar

    c) The status bar

    d) The title bar

2. **Which feature is used to display an active window and minimize all the other open windows?**

    a) Aero Flip

    b) Snap

    c) Aero Peek

    d) Shake

TOPIC D
Use Windows Help and Support

You worked with open windows to accomplish many Windows 7 tasks. Another important skill to acquire is the ability to obtain help information from within Windows 7. In this topic, you will use Windows Help and Support.

When you are unclear on how to accomplish a task or when there is an option or a tool that you want to find out more about, you can quickly access the information you need by using the Help and Support feature.

The Windows Help and Support Feature

The *Windows Help and Support* feature acts as a central location where you can learn how to get things done, solve problems, and obtain product support information. You can access this feature on the desktop by choosing **Help and Support** from the **Start** menu, or by pressing the Windows logo key along with **F1**. The **Windows Help and Support** home page groups common things you may want to know as a new user in three categories: **Find an answer quickly, Not sure where to start,** and **More on the Windows website.** You can also search for a particular term or a topic by entering the search query in the **Search Help** text box. You can also use specific tools that are found on the **Windows Help and Support** navigation bar.

To get help beyond the scope of topics on the **Windows Help and Support** home page, you can use the buttons on the navigation bar. The following table lists the different buttons on the navigation bar in the **Windows Help and Support** window.

Button	Description
The **Back** and **Forward** buttons	Help you navigate between the help pages you visited.
Help and Support Home	Returns you to the **Windows Help and Support** home page.
Print	Allows you to print the current help page.
Browse Help	Enables you to browse through help contents.
Ask	Enables you to get help from a friend or from a Microsoft support professional or to use a Windows website forum.
Options	Provides you with options to print, browse help contents, adjust text size, locate content on the same page, and change settings.

How to Use Windows Help and Support

Procedure Reference: Access Windows Help and Support

To access Windows Help and Support:

1. Open Windows Help and Support.
   - Click the **Start** button and choose **Help and Support.**
   - Or, on the keyboard, press **F1.**
2. In the **Search Help** text box, type the search query.
3. Click the **Search** button to begin the search.
4. Click the relevant link to view the information.
5. If necessary, click the **Help and Support home** icon to return to the home page of Windows Help and Support.

ACTIVITY 2-8
Accessing the Windows Help and Support Feature

Before You Begin:
The Windows 7 desktop is displayed with no other open programs.

Scenario:
Knowing a few important keyboard shortcuts will help you save your work time, and also speeds up your work. Aware of this advantage, you decide to seek information on keyboard shortcuts using the **Windows Help and Support** feature.

What You Do	How You Do It
1. Launch Windows Help and Support.	a. On the desktop, click the **Start** button to display the **Start** menu. b. On the **Start** menu, choose **Help and Support** to display the **Windows Help and Support** window. c. Maximize the **Windows Help and Support** window.
2. Search for information on keyboard shortcuts using Windows Help and Support.	a. In the **Search Help** text box, type *keyboard shortcuts* and click the **Search Help** button. b. In the displayed results, click the topic titled **Keyboard shortcuts** to view the relevant information. c. Close the **Windows Help and Support** window.

DISCOVERY ACTIVITY 2-9
Searching the Windows Help and Support Documents

Scenario:
You are in the process of troubleshooting a problem related to your monitor. You want to locate suitable support documentation.

1. **Which option enables you to locate content on the displayed help page?**
   a) The More on the Windows website link
   b) The Search Help text box
   c) The Options button on the navigation bar
   d) The Browse Help button on the navigation bar

2. **Which button on the navigation bar enables you to seek help from a Microsoft support professional or to use a Windows website forum?**
   a) The Ask button
   b) The Help and Support home button
   c) The Options button
   d) The Browse Help button

TOPIC E
Turn Off Personal Computers

You performed basic tasks in Windows 7. You need to shut down your computer after completing your work. In this topic, you will switch off your personal computer.

You may need to turn off or shut down your computer when, for instance, a person from your technical services department needs to install some new hardware, or maybe it is just time to leave for the day. By learning proper shutdown procedures, you will be able to end your work session and turn off your computer safely and securely.

The Shut Down Option

The *Shut down option* allows you to turn off your system in a secure manner. When the **Shut down** command is executed, the operating system ends all system-related programs as well as the power consumption. This ensures integrity of all system files and hardware safety. If you have a program opened, you will be prompted to save any unsaved information before it is closed.

The Switch User Option

The *Switch user option* enables multiple users to open working sessions on a system at the same time. You can access this option from the **Welcome** screen or from the **Shut down** options on the **Start** menu. If another user has an account on your computer and needs to use it, the **Switch User** option enables the other person to log on and use the computer, without closing your work. Each user account has its own storage locations and personal settings. When the second user completes his work, you can switch back to your session and resume your work.

The Log Off Option

The *Log off option* enables you to end your working session without turning off the computer. This secures the system and your personal data. Logging off closes all open windows. To log on again, select your user account and enter your password.

The Lock Option

The *Lock option* enables you to secure your working session if you need to leave your computer for a short period of time. When a system is locked, all the open programs and documents remain in their working state, but only the **Welcome** screen is displayed. To resume working with the computer, you need to enter your password again to unlock the system.

The Restart Option

The *Restart option* enables you to reload Windows 7 and refresh your system's memory without turning off the computer or switching it on. A restart can help if programs stop responding because your computer is running low on memory. Sometimes, installing or uninstalling a program may also require you to restart the system.

The Sleep Option

The *Sleep option* puts the system in the power-saving mode. When the **Sleep** command is executed, the system saves the state of the desktop and any open documents and programs to its memory. It also turns off most peripherals, thereby reducing its power consumption. This can help to increase battery life if you are working on a portable system. To wake the system from the sleep state, move the mouse or press a key on the keyboard. The system returns to full functionality and allows you to resume working.

How to Turn Off Personal Computers

Procedure Reference: Shut Down the Computer

To shut down the computer:

1. Display the **Start** menu.
2. On the **Start** menu, click **Shut down** to shut down the system.

Procedure Reference: Switch Between Users

To switch between users:

1. Choose **Start→Shut down→Switch user.**
2. On the **Welcome** screen, log on as a different user.
   a. Click to select a user account.
   b. If necessary, enter the password.

 You can also click the **Switch User** button if you need to select a different user name.

Procedure Reference: Log Off the System

To log off the system:

1. Display the **Start** menu.
2. Choose **Shut down→Log off.**

Procedure Reference: Lock the System

To lock the system:

1. Display the **Start** menu.
2. Choose **Shut down→Lock** to lock the system.

Procedure Reference: Put the System in the Sleep Mode

To put the system in the **Sleep** mode:
1. Display the **Start** menu.
2. Choose **Shut down→Sleep.**

ACTIVITY 2-10
Shutting Down the Computer

Before You Begin:
The Windows 7 desktop is displayed with no open windows.

Scenario:
You are done with the day's work. Before leaving, you want to shut down your computer.

What You Do	How You Do It
1. Shut down the computer.	a. On the desktop, click the **Start** button to display the **Start** menu.
	b. On the **Start** menu, hover the mouse pointer over the arrow beside the **Shut down** button to view the different power options.
	c. Click the **Shut down** button to shut down the computer.
	d. Observe that the text "Shutting down" is displayed.

2. **Under which of these situations will you restart a computer?**

   a) When another user has to log on to the system

   b) When a program is not responding to your commands

   c) When the system is to be awakened from its Sleep state

   d) When a day's work is done

   e) When a program is installed on your computer

DISCOVERY ACTIVITY 2-11
Identifying the Shut Down Options

Scenario:
You need to share your computer with a colleague. You also want to handle your working sessions effectively with the same computer. You decide to examine the different shut down options and determine the best option for a given scenario.

1. You have a meeting to attend and your colleague will also attend the meeting with you. However, you will return to your workstation within a short while and resume your current working session. Which power option will you choose?

    a) The Log off option

    b) The Lock option

    c) The Switch user option

    d) The Shut down option

2. What happens when a system is in the Sleep state?

    a) All open documents are saved, applications remain in the same state, and the system moves into a paused state.

    b) Your working session gets terminated.

    c) All open applications are closed and the system moves into a paused state.

    d) The user is prompted to save files and the system moves into a paused state.

Lesson 2 Follow-up

In this lesson, you logged on to Windows 7, explored its environment, and identified components that constitute the user interface. Understanding these components is essential before you start performing more complex tasks in Windows 7.

1. **In your opinion, which of the Aero features in Windows 7 are user-friendly? Why?**

2. **In which situations do you think, you are most likely to use the Windows 7 Help system?**

3 Managing Folders and Files

Lesson Time: 55 minutes

Lesson Objectives:

In this lesson, you will manage files and folders using Windows Explorer to navigate to folders and manage files.

You will:

- Navigate to folders using Windows Explorer to access files and folders quickly.
- Organize folders and files using Windows Explorer for better file management operations.
- Copy data on storage media using the data backup feature to create a backup of the data.

Introduction

You explored the Windows 7 desktop and worked with several windows. Once you begin to create files on your PC, it is necessary to manage them as well. In this lesson, you will manage folders and files.

Imagine that you have spent the last 20 minutes scanning through piles of papers at your office desk for a presentation you wrote a week ago. You need it for a meeting that will begin in the next five minutes. If only you had all your papers neatly organized in a folder within a filing cabinet, you would not have ended up in this situation. Your computer is not much different than your desk. Keeping your files well organized on your computer can help prevent a similar situation.

TOPIC A
Navigate to Folders with Windows Explorer

You worked with open windows and arranged them to suit your preferences. To access and store data on your system, you will need a tool that enables you to view and manage your files and folders. In this topic, you will navigate to folders with Windows Explorer components.

The Windows hierarchical structure might not be of much use to you if you do not know how to navigate in it. Windows Explorer gives you a bird's-eye view of your system's folder and file organization and enables you to navigate through the hierarchical structure. Working effectively with Windows Explorer is an important requirement to maintain an organized computer system.

Files

Definition:

A file is an object that contains user data for document files, or program codes for application files. All data on your computer is stored in files of various types. A file has a name and an extension. The nature of a file may vary depending on the application with which it is associated. Files are classified into two types—system and user files. The operating system and other applications run using system files. On the other hand, user files are created and managed by users.

 User files can be deleted or modified; however, these functions cannot be done on system files because any modification or deletion of an application's system file can affect its functionality.

Example:

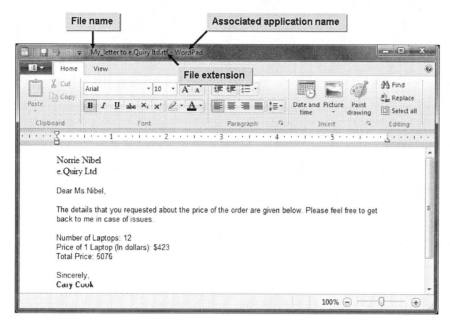

Figure 3-1: A WordPad file in Windows 7 displaying the file name and file extension.

File Extensions

File extensions refer to the format of a file and its type. Windows 7 uses the file extension to identify the program that is associated with a file. When you try to open the file, it is opened in the associated application. File extensions are not always visible within applications or utilities in Windows 7. You can customize your folder settings in such a way that you can view file extensions.

Folders

Definition:

A *folder* is a container that can store files in an organized manner. By default, a folder is represented by a folder icon. Folders can be of different types and can contain any number of other folders and files, including pictures, images, music, videos, documents, or a mix of any of these types. A folder is also referred to as a directory.

Example:

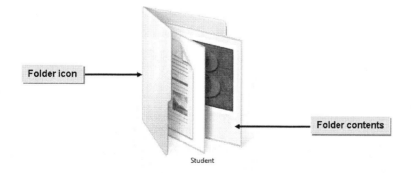

Figure 3-2: A folder containing files in Windows 7.

Subfolders and Their Features

A folder within a folder is called a subfolder. In a hierarchical folder display, folders that contain subfolders have a right-pointing arrow beside them. Clicking this arrow will expand the directory structure inside that folder.

Folder and File Naming Conventions

When you save a document as a file, it is important to name it appropriately. Naming a folder or a file according to a logical scheme enables you to organize your data properly.

Guidelines

When you name a folder or file, be sure to:

- Use a name that indicates the content or purpose of the document, project, or task to which it is related.
- Limit the length of the name. Though 260 characters can be used, file names of this length are impractical.
- Avoid using special characters. The backslash (\ ), forward slash (/), vertical bar (|), colon (:), asterisk (*), question mark (?), quotation mark ("), less than (<), and greater than (>) characters are not permitted.

Example:

If you are using WordPad to create a letter to send to your friends and family around the holidays, you might name the file HolidayLet2009.doc so that you will be able to identify the file without having to read its contents.

Windows Explorer

Windows Explorer is a system navigation tool that displays a structured and hierarchical view of your entire system in a double-paned window. It allows you to access all your local and network resources. You can also use Windows Explorer to manage information on your computer by copying and moving files.

The Explorer window is divided into several sections: the top panel, the navigation pane, the file list section, and the details pane. The top panel includes the navigation buttons, the address bar, the **Refresh** button, the **Search** text box, and the command bar. Two other sections that are not displayed by default in Windows Explorer are the preview pane and the menu bar. You can enable them, if required. The preview pane allows you to preview files and the menu bar provides additional menus to perform common tasks.

The Separator Bar

The vertical line between the panes is called the separator bar. It may be necessary at times to increase or decrease the size of a pane so that you can view more of the hierarchy. For example, to widen the left pane, position the mouse pointer on the separator bar. When the mouse pointer becomes a horizontal two-headed arrow, drag it to the right to widen the left pane.

Expanding and Collapsing the Windows Hierarchical Structure

In addition to adjusting the separator bar, you can also navigate by expanding and collapsing the Windows hierarchical structure. In the **Folders** list, a right-pointing arrow is displayed in front of a folder to indicate that the folder contains other folders in it. An arrow pointing to the lower-right indicates that the folder is already expanded and cannot be expanded any further. If an arrow is not displayed, the folder has no other folders inside it, and its contents are shown in the right pane. To expand a folder, click its arrow sign. To collapse a folder, click the arrow that points to the lower-right. In the left pane, you can also click the object to either expand a collapsed object or collapse an expanded object. Additionally, clicking the object will also display its contents in the right pane.

Libraries

The *Libraries* folder is used to manage your documents, music, pictures, and other files. You can browse files the same way as you would browse a folder. However, unlike a folder, a library collects files that are stored in different locations. Libraries don't actually store files, but monitor folders that contain files, and let you access and arrange items in different ways. For instance, if you have images in folders on your hard disk and on an external drive, you can access all these images at once using the **Pictures** library. Windows has four default libraries, **Documents, Music, Pictures,** and **Videos.** You can also create new libraries. Within each library, you can choose locations from where the files in the library get displayed and also arrange files based on their attributes.

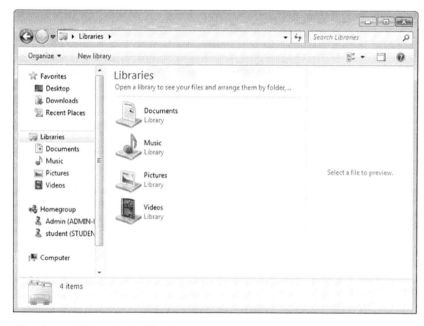

Figure 3-3: *The default libraries in Windows 7.*

The Windows File and Folder Hierarchy

In Windows 7, objects such as folders and other containers, files, and shortcuts are hierarchically structured at several levels so that they can be organized logically. Objects can be stored to any number of such hierarchical levels similar to a folder containing many subfolders and a subfolder containing any number of folders and files. The left pane in Windows Explorer generally displays the folder hierarchy.

Introduction to Personal Computers Using Windows® 7

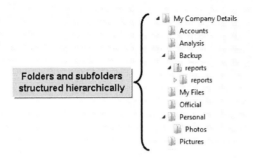

Figure 3-4: Folders and subfolders displayed in a hierarchical structure.

The Windows Explorer Components

The Windows Explorer components help you explore the Windows hierarchy and work with data.

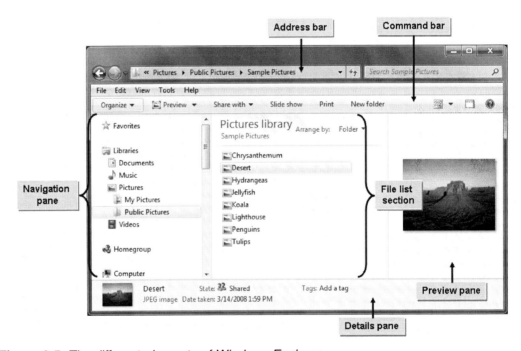

Figure 3-5: The different elements of Windows Explorer.

The Windows Explorer elements are described in the following table.

Component	Description
The address bar	Is located below the title bar of a window. It displays the address of an object. It includes the breadcrumbs and address path views. The breadcrumbs view is enabled by default and makes it easier to navigate through files and folders. You can click the small arrows next to each folder to list the subfolders within it. You can navigate to any of the subfolders by clicking them. The address path view enables you to type an object's address to access it. You can switch between these two views by clicking the address bar. When you select another item, it switches back to the breadcrumbs view.
The navigation pane	Is located in the left pane of the window. It enables you to scroll and directly access folders. The navigation pane contains two sections: the **Favorites** section and the **Folders list.** The **Favorites** section provides links to the **Desktop, Downloads, Recent Places,** and **Searches.** The **Folders list** is dynamic and automatically positions the tree structure to help you view the folder hierarchy easily, while you navigate. You can also choose to hide the **Folders list.**
The command bar	Is displayed below the address bar. It is contextual and dynamic. It can show a list of common tasks depending upon the selected object or objects. By default, it contains two buttons: **Organize** and **Views.** The **Organize** button consists of options for basic folder management. The **Views** button allows you to click or drag its slider to change the file list view. When files are listed in the **File List** section, the command bar displays buttons for performing tasks related to these file types. It also allows you to perform common tasks such as opening, printing, and sharing files.
The **File List** section	Is located in the right pane of the window. It displays a list of files and subfolders within a folder. It consists of column headings that help in arranging contents in various categories such as name, size, and type of file.
The preview pane	Is located to the right of the **File List** section. It enables you to preview files such as documents, presentation slides, and images without opening them in an application. It displays the actual file content rather than a thumbnail or an icon. You can also play music and video files in the preview pane.

Component	Description
The details pane	Is located at the bottom of the window, and displays file properties such as file name, file type, author, last modified, size, and other properties. You can also add or modify the properties of a file and save the file from the details pane. In addition, you can rate the quality of files such as music, picture, and videos. When you increase the size of the details pane, it displays the additional properties that are associated with the selected file.

How to Navigate to Folders with Windows Explorer

Procedure Reference: Navigate to Folders

To navigate to a desired folder:

1. If necessary, display Windows Explorer.
2. Navigate to the desired folder.
   - In the left pane displaying the **Folders list,** expand the master folder and click the desired folder to view its contents in the right pane.
   - Or, in the address bar, click the arrow beside a link and from the displayed drop-down list, select the desired folder.
3. Double-click the folder to view its contents.

Introduction to Personal Computers Using Windows® 7

ACTIVITY 3-1
Navigating to Folders Using Windows Explorer

Before You Begin:
The Windows 7 desktop is displayed with no open programs.

Scenario:
Your colleague wants you to demonstrate the features of the Windows Explorer tool and explain how it can help in navigating hierarchically. You also decide to demonstrate how to change the display of contents.

What You Do	How You Do It
1. Navigate to folders using Windows Explorer.	a. On the taskbar, click the **Windows Explorer** icon to launch Windows Explorer.
	b. If necessary, maximize the **Windows Explorer** window.
	c. Observe that the **Libraries** folder and its contents are displayed.
	d. In the right pane, double-click the **Pictures** library.
	e. In the **Pictures library,** double-click the **Sample Pictures** folder to view the files.
2. Use the breadcrumbs view to navigate to different locations.	a. On the address bar, click the arrow to the right of the **Libraries** link and from the displayed drop-down list, select **Videos.**
	b. To the left of the address bar, click the **Back** button to return to the **Sample Pictures** folder.
	c. On the address bar, click the **Pictures** link to return to the **Pictures** folder.

Lesson 3: Managing Folders and Files 85

3.	Expand and collapse the folder hierarchy.	a.	In the navigation pane, select **Libraries** to display the default Windows 7 libraries in the right pane.
		b.	In the navigation pane, click the arrow beside **Music** to expand the folder.
		c.	Click the arrow beside **Public Music** to expand the folder.
		d.	Select the **Sample Music** folder to view the files.
		e.	Click the arrow beside **Music** to collapse the folder.
4.	Change the display settings of the libraries.	a.	On the command bar, to the right of the **Views** button, click the drop-down arrow.
		b.	Click and drag the slider to **Extra Large Icons.**
		c.	Observe that the icons become larger in size.
		d.	On the command bar, to the right of the **Views** button, click the drop-down arrow.
		e.	Click and drag the slider back to the previous view, which is, the **Details** view.
		f.	Close Windows Explorer.

DISCOVERY ACTIVITY 3-2
Exploring the Windows Explorer Components

Scenario:
You have explored the user interface and examined the tools and applications available in Windows 7. Before you start working, you want to examine the Windows Explorer components and understand how folders and files are organized.

---

1. Which sections are not displayed by default in Windows Explorer? (Choose two.)
    a) The command bar
    b) The preview pane ✓
    c) The details pane
    d) The menu bar ✓
    e) The address bar

2. Where can you view file information and add properties to a file?
    a) The address bar
    b) The details pane ✓
    c) The preview pane
    d) The navigation pane

TOPIC B
Work with Folders and Files

You explored the components of Windows Explorer and identified how you can use them to navigate in a hierarchical system. Now that you can navigate within Windows Explorer, you are better able to perform folder and file management operations. In this topic, you will work with folders and files.

As you work, you may need to create, organize, copy, or delete files. Although the Windows Explorer window is quite intuitive in the way it is organized, you will find it easier to work with it if you master the basic techniques of creating, cutting, copying, and pasting objects.

Folder and File Shortcuts

A shortcut is a pointer object that enables you to open the frequently used files, folders, or applications. By default, Windows 7 provides you with various shortcuts. Items on the **Start** menu are just shortcuts that point to the executable files of their respective programs. Creating shortcuts on the desktop enables you to access objects immediately when you log on to the computer.

Figure 3-6: The desktop displaying shortcuts to a folder and a file.

Basic Folder and File Management

Basic folder and file management actions can be performed in any Windows Explorer window.

The following table describes the folder and file management actions that can be performed in Windows Explorer.

Action	Description
Create objects	When you create a folder or a file, you need to decide where to store it in the overall Windows hierarchy. You can create folders and files on the desktop or on any drive, though it is recommended that you confine your data to the Documents folder. You can also create new files and folders within existing folders. This is called nesting folders.
Select multiple objects	In Windows Explorer, you can select several objects at the same time as long as they are located in the same location. Being able to select multiple files, for instance, is handy if you want to rename, copy, or move many of them in one single action. These objects may be listed next to each other (contiguous) or they may be separated by other objects that you do not want to select (noncontiguous). • To select contiguous objects, click the first one and then press **Shift** while you click the last one. • To select noncontiguous objects, press **Ctrl** while you click each one. • To select everything in a container, choose **Edit→Select All** or press **Ctrl+A.**
Rename objects	As you create and manage folders and files, you may at some point want to rename them. You can rename a file or folder by choosing **File→Rename.** You can also rename several objects at the same time. You can mix file types (you can rename word-processing files and picture files at the same time), you can rename files and folders at the same time, and you can also rename multiple folders at the same time.
Copy objects	Sometimes, you may want to duplicate a file or a folder and all of its contents, leaving the original intact. Perhaps you want to make a copy of important information in case you make a mistake while editing the original. You can make a copy of a folder and store it in a different location or in the same location as the original folder. If you make a copy in the same location, the name of the copy ends with "- Copy."

Action	Description
Move objects	If you accidentally create an object in the wrong location or if you just want to reorganize your folders, you can easily move the object or folders to any desired location.
Delete objects	When you do not require a file, folder, shortcut, or any such object any longer, you can either delete these items permanently, or move them to the **Recycle Bin** temporarily. This will help reduce clutter and retain only the files that you require and use. When deleting, ensure that you delete only the files that you have created and not the system or program files.
Undo last action	In Windows 7 and most Windows-based programs, if you ever make a mistake while moving, deleting, cutting, copying, pasting, or formatting folders, files, or text, you have an opportunity to undo the last action. For instance, if you move a file to the wrong location, and realize it immediately, you can choose **Edit→Undo Move.** The **Undo** action adjusts itself to reflect the last action performed. So, if the last thing you did was deleting a folder, the menu choice would be **Edit→ Undo Delete.**

Default Folder and File Names

If you create a new folder or a file object in Windows Explorer, it is given a default name depending on the nature of the object. For example, a new folder object would be named New Folder until you explicitly rename it. Each object within a container must have a unique name so that if you create additional folders in the same location, they will be named New Folder (2), New Folder (3), and so on. This applies to default file names as well.

Folder and File Properties

Folder and file properties are pieces of information about a folder or a file, other than its content, that are stored with them. When you create a folder or a file, the system records some unique properties such as the file creation date, file type, and file location. However, you can add other properties later, if required. The properties of a folder or a file can help you locate it easily and can be viewed from the details pane, a tooltip, or using the **Properties** dialog box. To view the additional properties of a file, you need to right-click the column headings and choose **More** and, in the **Choose Details** dialog box displayed, select the required details to view that property. The properties of a folder provide information about the number of files and folders contained within it.

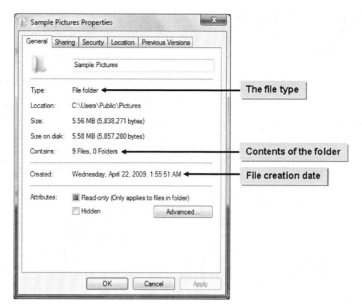

Figure 3-7: The Sample Properties dialog box displaying the properties of the Sample Pictures folder.

Personal Information

Personal information is the additional description that you provide for a file. Depending on the file type, you can add suitable values such as author name, title, rating, copyright, and company name. Unlike regular file properties, personal information can provide minute or sensitive details about a file. This also helps you organize or search your files more efficiently. You can add your personal information in categories such as **Description, Origin, Content,** and **File.** These categories will vary depending on the type of the file. It is better to remove your personal information before sharing it with others.

The Recycle Bin Options

The *Recycle Bin,* available on the desktop, provides you with options to open, empty its contents, rename, create a shortcut to the **Recycle Bin** and view its properties. If you choose the **Empty Recycle Bin** option from the shortcut menu, the files will be permanently deleted from the system. You can also restore files that were temporarily deleted. When you restore a file, the file automatically gets restored in the location where you first saved it.

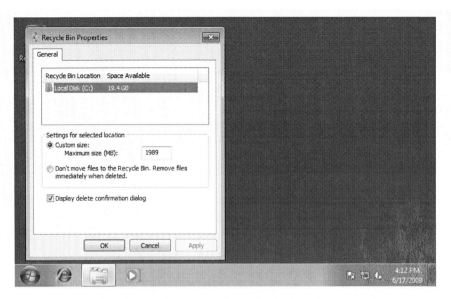

Figure 3-8: The Recycle Bin Properties dialog box displaying the Recycle Bin options.

Rules for Deletion

You should delete files only from folders that you create or from the Documents folder. You should not delete files or folders from any other location. Two folders that you should strictly avoid deleting are the Program Files and Windows folders. The Program Files folder is where Windows 7 installs your software, and the Windows folder is where the Windows 7 operating system resides. Modifying or deleting files from either of these folders can damage the programs or your PC. Therefore, follow this rule of thumb: Never access these two folders unless there is a need for them.

How to Work with Folders and Files

Procedure Reference: Create a Folder or File Within Windows Explorer

To create a folder or file within Windows Explorer:

1. Open Windows Explorer and navigate to the container where you want to create a folder or file.
2. Create the object.
    - Choose **File→New** and select the object type from the submenu.
    - Or, right-click in an empty space in the container, choose **New,** and select the object type from the submenu.
3. Type the name for the object.
4. Press **Enter** or click anywhere on the desktop to confirm the object name.

Procedure Reference: Rename a Folder or File

To rename a folder or file:

1. Locate and select the folder or file you want to rename.
2. Select the existing name to be overwritten.
    - Choose **File→Rename.**
    - Right-click the object and choose **Rename.**
    - Or, select the object and press **F2.**

3. Type the new name.
4. Press **Enter** or click anywhere on the desktop to confirm the new name.

Procedure Reference: Copy and Paste a Folder or File

To copy and paste a folder or file:
1. Locate and select the object you want to copy.
2. Copy the object.
   - On the menu bar, choose **Edit→Copy.**
   - On the menu bar, choose **Edit→Copy To Folder,** select a location where you want to place the copy, and click **Copy.**
   - Right-click the object and choose **Copy.**
   - Or, select the object and press **Ctrl+C.**
3. Paste the object in a new location.
   - Navigate to the desired location, and on the menu bar, choose **Edit→Paste.**
   - Navigate to the desired location, and in the **File List** section, right-click an empty location and then choose **Paste.**
   - Or, in the desired location, press **Ctrl+V.**

Procedure Reference: Move a Folder or File

To move a folder or file:
1. Locate and select the object you want to move.
2. Move the object to its new location.
   - Drag the object from its old location to the new location.
   - On the menu bar, choose **Edit→Move To Folder,** select a location where you want to move it, and click **Move.**
   - Right-click the original object, hold down the right mouse button, and drag the mouse pointer over the new location. When you release the mouse button, choose **Move Here.**
   - Cut the object and paste it into the new location.
3. If necessary, rename the object.

Procedure Reference: Use the Recycle Bin

To use the **Recycle Bin** to delete or restore files or folders:
1. Locate and select the objects you want to delete.
2. Move the objects to the **Recycle Bin.**
   - Press **Delete** and click **Yes** to send the objects to the **Recycle Bin.**
   - Right-click the object, choose **Delete,** and click **Yes** to send the object to the **Recycle Bin.**
   - Or, drag an object or selected objects to the **Recycle Bin.**
3. To restore a deleted object, open the **Recycle Bin,** select the object, and choose **File→ Restore,** or right-click the object and choose **Restore.** You can also drag the object to the desired location.

4. Delete objects from the **Recycle Bin** permanently.
   - Right-click the **Recycle Bin** icon and choose **Empty Recycle Bin.**
   - Open the **Recycle Bin** and choose **File→Empty Recycle Bin.**
   - Or, open the **Recycle Bin,** right-click an empty location in the right pane, and from the shortcut menu, choose **Empty Recycle Bin.**
5. Click **Yes** to confirm the deletion.

Procedure Reference: Create Shortcuts

To create a shortcut:
1. Locate and select the object for which you need to create a shortcut.
2. Specify the location of the shortcut.
   - To create a shortcut on the desktop, right-click the object and choose **Send to→Desktop (create shortcut).**
   - To create a shortcut in the same location as the original file, right-click the object and choose **Create Shortcut.**

You can also select the object, press and hold down **Alt,** and drag the mouse pointer away from the original object. When you release the mouse button, the shortcut will be created.

   - Or, right-click the original file and drag the mouse pointer to another location. When you release the mouse button, choose **Create Shortcuts Here.**
3. If necessary, move the shortcut to the new location. If you drag a folder shortcut to the **Start** menu, a folder shortcut is added to the **Pinned Items** list of the **Start** menu.

ACTIVITY 3-3
Managing Folders and Files

Before You Begin:
The Windows 7 desktop is displayed with no open programs.

Scenario:
You are aware that your system's Pictures folder contains some default pictures. All these pictures are likely to be modified for some other use. You want to store a copy of these pictures in a new folder that needs to be customized for managing picture files. Because you will be working with this folder frequently, you prefer to have this folder added to your **Favorites** list. Also, you decide to create a shortcut to this folder on the desktop to quickly access it.

What You Do	How You Do It
1. Create a folder.	a. Choose **Start→Computer**.
	b. On the command bar, choose **Organize→Layout→Menu bar** to display the menu bar.
	c. In the file list section, double-click the **Local Disk (C:)** icon.
	d. On the command bar, click **New folder** to create a folder.
	e. Type *My project* and press **Enter** to change the folder's name.

2.	Copy the contents of a folder to another location.	a.	In Windows Explorer, in the left pane, click **Pictures.**
		b.	In the right pane, double-click the **Sample Pictures** folder to display the files.
		c.	On the menu bar, choose **Edit→Select all** to select all the picture files.
		d.	Choose **Edit→Copy** to copy all the files to the clipboard.
		e.	In the left pane, hover the mouse pointer over the **Computer** link to display the navigation arrow.
		f.	Click the arrow beside **Computer** to expand the folder.
		g.	Click the arrow beside **Local Disk (C:)** to expand the folder.
		h.	From the **Local Disk (C:)** folder tree, click the **My project** folder.
		i.	On the menu bar, choose **Edit→Paste** to paste all the copied files into this folder.
		j.	In the left pane, collapse **Libraries.**
3.	Add a folder to the **Favorites** list and create a shortcut for the folder on the desktop.	a.	In the left pane, click and drag the **My project** folder to the **Favorites** list just below **Recent Places.**
		b.	In the **Favorites** list, right-click the **My project** folder to display the shortcut menu.
		c.	From the shortcut menu, choose **Send to→Desktop (create shortcut)** to create a shortcut to this folder on the desktop.
		d.	Close Windows Explorer.
4.	Rename a shortcut on the desktop.	a.	On the desktop, right-click the **My project** shortcut icon.
		b.	From the shortcut menu, choose **Rename** to rename the object.
		c.	Type *Project Backup* and click outside the icon border to deselect it.

ACTIVITY 3-4
Using the Recycle Bin

Before You Begin:
The Windows 7 desktop is displayed with no open programs.

Scenario:
The images that you backed up in the My project folder are not needed anymore and you want to discard the shortcut you created on the desktop. You also decide to delete the My project folder on the C drive. After discarding both the folders, one of your colleagues asks you to provide the same set of images for his use.

What You Do	How You Do It
1. Delete the unnecessary folder.	a. On the desktop, right-click the **Project Backup** shortcut and choose **Delete**.
	b. In the **Delete Shortcut** message box, click **Yes** to confirm the file deletion.
	c. From the taskbar, launch Windows Explorer.
	d. In the **Folders list** section, click **Local Disk (C:)**.
	e. In the right pane, right-click the **My project** folder and choose **Delete** to display the **Delete Folder** message box.
	f. In the **Delete Folder** message box, click **Yes** to confirm the folder deletion.
	g. Close Windows Explorer.

2. Restore a deleted item and empty the **Recycle Bin**.

   a. On the desktop, double-click the **Recycle Bin** icon to display the deleted contents.

   b. In the **Recycle Bin** window, right-click the **My project** folder and choose **Restore**.

   c. On the command bar, click **Empty the Recycle Bin**.

   d. In the **Delete File** message box, click **Yes** to empty the **Recycle Bin**.

   e. Close the **Recycle Bin** window.

DISCOVERY ACTIVITY 3-5
Working with Folders and Files

Scenario:
As a part of your day-to-day activities, you frequently need to perform varied tasks with files and folders. You want to familiarize yourself with the basic file and folder management techniques.

1. Which option deletes files permanently from the system?

    a) Delete

    (b) Empty Recycle Bin

    c) Restore

    d) Create a Shortcut

2. **True or False? The Favorites list provides a shortcut to the user's desktop.**

    X True

    ___ False

TOPIC C
Copy Data on Storage Media

You managed files and folders stored on your hard disk. You need to perform some special tasks with files and folders on removable media such as CD or DVD storage devices. In this topic, you will copy files to storage devices such as a DVD.

No matter how many copies of the same file you have in different places on your local disk, a hard disk crash could erase all your data completely. To prevent such losses and also to have a more dependable backup of your data, you can copy files onto external storage media such as CDs or DVDs. Windows 7 provides an easy way to copy files to any writable storage device using a simple copying process.

Data Backup

Data backup refers to copying your files from one location on your computer to a different location or to a removable storage device, such as a floppy disk, CD, or DVD. These additional copies may be used to restore the original files if there is any loss in the primary data. Data backup helps to restore the files which have been accidentally deleted or corrupted.

How to Copy Data on Storage Media

Procedure Reference: Copy Pictures to a CD or DVD

To copy pictures to a CD or DVD:

1. If necessary, install a writable CD or DVD drive on your system.
2. Insert the CD or DVD into the writer.

Using a CD writer, you can only copy data onto a CD. But by using a DVD writer, you can copy data onto both CDs and DVDs.

3. Navigate to the location that contains the data to be copied.
4. In Windows Explorer, on the command bar, choose **Organize→Select all.**
5. On the command bar, click the **Burn** button.
6. In the **Burn to Disc** wizard, in the **Disc title** text box, enter a title name and click **Next.**

The writing speed depends on the data size and your device settings. You may also select multiple files to be copied at the same time.

7. When the burn process is complete, click **Finish** to close the **Burn to Disc** wizard.
8. If necessary, navigate to the CD/DVD drive and check if the data is properly copied.

ACTIVITY 3-6
Copying a File to a DVD

Before You Begin:
A DVD writer is installed on your system and a DVD is inserted into it.

Scenario:
You want to deliver a presentation about your company to a set of new employees. You want to add some pictures on the slides and you want to save a copy of the pictures on a DVD so that you can work on the presentation at home.

What You Do	How You Do It
1. Select the file to be copied.	a. Choose **Start→Pictures** to open the **Pictures Library**.
	b. In the **Pictures library,** double-click the **Sample Pictures** folder to open it.
	c. On the command bar, choose **Organize→Select all** to select all the images.
2. Copy the selected files to the DVD.	a. On the command bar, click **Burn.**
	b. In the **Burn a Disc** wizard, in the **Disc title** text box, type *Sample Pictures* and click **Next.**
	c. Observe that the **Burn a Disc** wizard indicates that the burn process is in progress.
	d. If necessary, verify that the files are copied to the DVD and close the DVD RW Drive window.
	e. Close Windows Explorer.

DISCOVERY ACTIVITY 3-7
Examining Data Backup Options

Scenario:
You have prepared a tax report on your business expenses and losses. You need to file this report with the tax authorities. You decide to make a backup of this report on a CD and start examining data backup options.

1. You have selected a sample picture that you want to burn to a CD. Which option will you choose to display the Burn a Disc wizard to begin the CD burning process?

    a) Burn→DVD.

    b) Burn→CD.

    c) File→Burn.

    d) Burn→Data Disc.

2. True or False? You can make a backup of your files only from your computer to a removable storage device such as a CD.

    ___ True

    ___ False

Lesson 3 Follow-up

In this lesson, you managed folders and files. You familiarized yourself with the Windows hierarchy. You also explored, and created folder and file objects. In addition to this, you searched data and used the **Recycle Bin** effectively. With these skills, you can easily keep your files and folders organized so that you can access information quickly whenever you need it.

1. **How can a properly organized file and folder structure help you access and manage data efficiently?**

2. **How can making a backup of your data help in your work setup?**

4 Using Common Tools and Programs

Lesson Time: 1 hour(s), 20 minutes

Lesson Objectives:

In this lesson, you will understand application software, and use common tools and applications that are part of the Windows 7 operating system such as the WordPad word processor, the Paint tool, the Calculator tool, among others.

You will:

- Examine the various categories of application software to use them for various business needs.

- Create a document using WordPad to perform tasks such as moving, copying, and pasting text.

- Perform simple calculations using the Calculator to obtain mathematical results.

- Customize a graphic using the Paint tool to modify it according to your requirements.

Introduction

You explored the Windows 7 environment and managed folders and files. Now, you can begin performing your everyday computing tasks, and in the process, you may use simple tools such as a text editor, the Calculator, or the Paint program that help handle some basic tasks. You might also use the application software to perform specific tasks. In this lesson, you will work with some of the common tools and programs.

In the course of your work, you may be required to draft a letter, do a small calculation, modify an image, or perform other computing tasks. These are some simple tasks you might have to carry out on a regular basis. Windows 7 provides you with a set of programs that you can use to accomplish these tasks with ease. However, there are various other programs available that can be used to perform many other tasks. Becoming familiar with these programs will enable you to handle your primary office tasks efficiently.

TOPIC A
Examine Application Software

You managed folders and files. Now, you are ready to work with the software to accomplish your tasks. In this topic, you will examine the various categories of the application software.

Every user's software needs are different. The needs might be related to web browsing, development tools, image editing programs, or communication programs. Based upon your individual requirements, application software can be installed on your computer.

Application Software

Definition:

A *software application* is a program that helps you perform specific tasks in the processing or manipulation of data. Each application provides instructions to a computer and these instructions are used to control how the computer will process data. The manner in which these instructions are applied depends on the commands you give to the application using various input devices.

Example:

Typical application software programs include word processors, databases, and spreadsheets. Most application programs have been designed for a specific use but often include features that enable you to use them for other purposes as well.

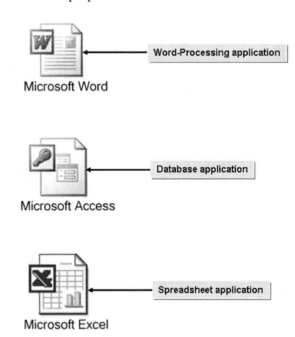

Figure 4-1: Common application software programs installed on a personal computer.

Categories of Application Software

There are various categories of application software that are designed for a specific purpose. Word processors are used for creating letters, memos, reports, and other documents, while spreadsheets are used for managing, calculating, and analyzing tables of numbers. Presentations are used for creating graphical representations, paper handouts, and projected presentations for conferences and meetings. Databases are used for managing extensive lists of information. There are other applications and utilities that allow you to view content on the web and perform file and system maintenance tasks.

Examples of Applications

A web browser allows you to view and interact with content on the Internet. You can also create, send, and receive email and manage your contact information using email clients. Additionally, you can manage your files and system on the hard drive using different utilities. The following table lists a few of the applications and the popular examples of each application that are used in day-to-day work by many professionals.

Application	*Examples Include*
Word processors	- Corel WordPerfect - Lotus Word Pro - Microsoft Office Word
Spreadsheets	- Corel Quattro Pro - Lotus 1-2-3 - Microsoft Office Excel
Presentations	- Corel Presentations - Lotus Freelance - Microsoft Office PowerPoint
Databases	- Corel Paradox - Lotus Approach - Microsoft Office Access
Web browsers	- Microsoft Internet Explorer - Mozilla Firefox - Netscape Navigator - Google Chrome

Word Processors

Definition:

A *word processor* is a computer application that is used to compose, edit, format, and print text. Word processors have a wide range of formatting options, tools, and settings that you can use to make your text more readable and attractive.

Example:

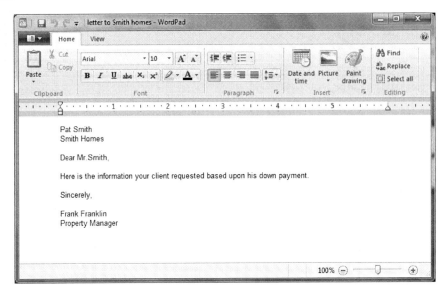

Figure 4-2: The WordPad program that is used compose, edit, format, and print text.

ACTIVITY 4-1
Choosing the Right Application

Scenario:
Your friend, James, works in a real estate company. His job involves sending brochures and price quotations to clients. He needs to use the correct application to get the optimum output.

1. **James wants to type a letter and send it to a client. Which application will be best suited for this job?**

    a) A spreadsheet

    b) A database

    c) A word processor

    d) Presentation software

2. **After typing the letter, James wants to modify the company logo and insert it in the letter. Which application can he use for this work?**

    a) A word processor

    b) A database

    c) Presentation software

    d) A graphics application

3. **True or False? James needs to prepare handouts containing charts and bulleted lists. He can accomplish this using a spreadsheet application.**

    ___ True

    ___ False

4. **James needs to record and maintain a list of clients' names, contact details, price quotations, and other details related to transactions. Which application software will you recommend to accomplish this task?**

    a) A web browser

    b) A word processor

    c) A database

    d) Presentation software

TOPIC B
Create a Document in WordPad

You examined the various categories of common application software. Now, you are ready to work with simple and commonly used applications in Windows 7. Possibly, the most commonly used software in both personal and professional environments is a word-processing application such as WordPad. In this topic, you will create a document in the WordPad application and save it.

Creating documents with a typewriter used to be a cumbersome process. You needed to load paper, adjust it, and type the contents; you could not easily make a file copy or an extra copy for another recipient. Making corrections in the document was not easy because it used up a lot of paper. Even with the advent of PCs and word processors, creating a document and saving it has never been so easy. WordPad is a simple word-processing application built into Windows 7 that is very easy to learn. You can use WordPad to create letters and memos without purchasing and installing any additional software.

WordPad

WordPad is a simple word-processing application that has basic formatting tools. It is included in most versions of the Microsoft Windows operating systems. It is more advanced than the Notepad application, but not as advanced as Microsoft Word. It has options to format and print text, but does not have tools such as **Spell Check** and **Thesaurus.** It supports the Rich Text Format (.rtf) that is compatible with Microsoft Word's file format (.doc). However, you cannot save a WordPad file in a .doc format. You can save it as text or rich text.

The Ribbon

The Ribbon is a panel located at the top of a WordPad document. It contains a selection of easy-to-browse commands that you may need to work on a document. The Ribbon has two tabs organized in the order in which they will be used during document creation. These tabs are divided into groups containing features that are designed to perform specific tasks during the authoring process. You can hide the Ribbon by double-clicking any active tab.

Tabs on the Ribbon

The Ribbon in WordPad consists of two tabs—**Home** and **View.** The **Home** tab contains options to copy, paste, format, insert, and edit elements in a WordPad document. The **View** tab lets you view a document in different views, show or hide components of the document window, wrap text in the document for readability, and provide measuring units for the ruler in the document window.

The Quick Access Toolbar

By default, the *Quick Access toolbar* is displayed at the top-left corner of the WordPad window, above the Ribbon. It provides easy access to core commands such as save, undo, and repeat. You can customize this toolbar to include other options based on user requirements. The **Quick Access** toolbar can also be placed below the Ribbon.

Text Selection Techniques

There are various text selection techniques that can help you select text when you want to copy, move, or change its appearance.

The following table describes the different text selection techniques available in Windows 7 applications.

Text Selection Technique	*Description*
Drag	Place the I-beam at the beginning of the text to be selected. Press and hold down the left mouse button. Move the mouse pointer to the other end of the text. This creates a highlighted area (a selection) between the two ends. Then, release the mouse button.
Select a word	Point anywhere inside the word and double-click. The trailing space is automatically selected along with the word.
Select a line	Point next to the line that you want to select in the left margin of the text area. The mouse pointer will change from an I-beam to a right-pointing arrow. Click the mouse button to select entire text on that line.
Select a paragraph	Point anywhere inside a paragraph and triple-click the mouse button. The paragraph is automatically selected.
Extend a selection	Make a selection. While pressing **Shift,** click beyond the selection. The selection extends to that point.
Select a document	Click **Select all** in the **Editing** group, or press **Ctrl+A.**

Deselecting a Selection

You can deselect an existing selection by making another selection or by clicking away from the selection area. This will undo the existing selection.

How to Create a Document in WordPad

Procedure Reference: Create and Save a Document in WordPad with Default Options

To create and save a document in WordPad:

1. Choose **Start→All Programs→Accessories→WordPad.**
2. In the document area, type your text.

   a. Click a location in the document area to place the insertion point.

    By default, when you open a document, the cursor is placed at the start of the page.

   b. Type the text. You can allow WordPad to wrap the text automatically to the next line.

   c. If necessary, press **Enter** to end a paragraph and start a new paragraph from the next line.

3. Display the **Save As** dialog box to save the document.
   - On the **Quick Access** toolbar, click the **Save** button.
   - Click the **WordPad** button and choose **Save.**
   - Or, press **Ctrl+S.**

4. If necessary, choose the desired options in the **Save As** dialog box.
   - Navigate to the desired location where you want to save the file.
   - In the **File name** text box, specify the desired name for the file.
   - From the **Save as type** drop-down list, select the desired format in which you want to save the file.

5. Click **Save** to save the document.

The Save As Dialog Box

The **Ctrl+S** command and the **Save** option on the **WordPad** menu and the **Quick Access** toolbar will display the **Save As** dialog box only when you save a document for the first time. After saving the document, when you reopen it to make changes and save it again, the **Save As** dialog box will not be displayed. However, you can choose the **Save as** option on the **WordPad** menu to save an existing document with a new name or in another location.

Saving a File

It is necessary to save a file because until you save your document, it exists only in the computer memory, which is a temporary storage. For permanent storage, you must save the document to a storage location such as the My Documents folder on your computer's hard drive. After saving the file for the first time, it is a good practice to continue to save your work frequently whenever you make changes. That way, if something happens to the file when it is open in memory, you will have a recent copy of the file on disk. This keeps your retyping to a minimum. Also, most programs will prompt you to save changes when you try to exit the program, thus preventing you from losing any update. The **Save** command updates the original file by saving changes under the same name and to the same location.

Procedure Reference: Open an Existing WordPad Document

To open an existing WordPad document:

1. Navigate to the location where the document is saved.
2. Open the document.
   - Double-click the document icon.
   - Right-click the document icon and choose **Open.**
   - Right-click the document icon and choose **Open With→WordPad.**
   - Or, open the document by using the WordPad program.
     a. Display the **Open** dialog box.
        - Click the **WordPad** button and choose **Open.**
        - Or, press **Ctrl+O.**
     b. If necessary, navigate to the location where the document is saved.
     c. Select the document.
     d. Click **Open.**

Opening a New WordPad Document

If you have the **WordPad** icon pinned to your taskbar, you can right-click it and choose the **WordPad** option from the jump list to open a new WordPad document.

ACTIVITY 4-2
Creating a WordPad Document

Before You Begin:
1. Navigate to the C:\084705Data folder, open the Letter.txt file in Notepad, and minimize the Notepad window.
2. Close Windows Explorer.

Scenario:
You are the property manager of a real-estate agency. You want to write an official letter to Mr. Pat Smith, a lawyer, regarding the information his client has requested.

What You Do	How You Do It
1. Create a WordPad document.	a. Choose **Start→All Programs→Accessories→WordPad** to open a blank document.
	b. If necessary, maximize the WordPad window.
	c. In the blank area, type **Pat Smith** and press **Enter.**
	d. Type **Smith Homes** and press **Enter.**
	e. On the taskbar, click the **Notepad** icon.
	f. In the **Letter.txt - Notepad** window, choose **Edit→Select All.**
	g. Choose **Edit→Copy.**
	h. Navigate to the **Document - WordPad** window.
	i. On the **Home** tab, in the **Clipboard** group, click the **Paste** button.

2. Save the document.

    a. Click the **WordPad** button and hover the mouse pointer over the **Save as** option.

    b. In the **Save a copy of the document** section, select the **Rich Text document** option.

    c. In the **Save As** dialog box, navigate to the C:\084705Data folder.

    d. In the **File name** text box, click and type *Letter to Smith Homes*

    e. Click **Save.**

    f. Observe that the title bar of the document now displays the name of the document.

    g. Close the **Letter to Smith Homes.rtf - WordPad** window.

    h. Close the **Letter.txt - Notepad** window.

DISCOVERY ACTIVITY 4-3
Working with WordPad

Scenario:
Your work involves typing business correspondence letters. You want to familiarize yourself with the WordPad application and the options it provides.

1. Which tab in the WordPad window lets you copy, paste, format, edit, and insert elements in a document?

    a) Home

    b) View

    c) Format

    d) Insert

2. True or False? By default, the Quick Access toolbar is located below the WordPad Ribbon.

    ___ True

    ___ False

TOPIC C
Work with the Calculator

You created and saved a document in WordPad. In addition to creating a text document, your job might also require that you perform arithmetic calculations. In this topic, you will use the **Calculator** tool to perform basic calculations and then copy the calculations to a WordPad document.

Consider a situation where you have a complex math problem to do, but you do not have a calculator in hand. Windows 7 provides a computerized calculator, which is quite similar to a handheld calculator. With it, you can solve simple math problems as well as perform complex scientific operations. The results from this can be copied to a WordPad.

The Calculator

The *Calculator* in Windows 7 is a program that is similar to a handheld calculator. It is used for solving math problems. It can be accessed from the **Accessories** submenu and consists of four views. In the **Standard** view, you can use this application to perform basic arithmetic calculations such as addition, subtraction, multiplication, and division. In the **Scientific** view, you can perform basic operations and functions such as logarithms and cosines.

The **Programmer** view of the **Calculator** lets you perform binary and decimal calculations and the **Statistics** view lets you perform statistical calculations. The **View** menu of the **Calculator** includes options for unit conversion and date calculation. You can also use the built-in worksheets to calculate your mortgage payments, vehicle lease, and gas mileage. Additionally, you can also view a history of calculations made earlier and edit them to get new results.

When you click a button in the **Calculator** window, it performs the button's corresponding function. The function may include entering a number or an operator, or correcting or clearing the numeric display. A few of the important buttons in the **Calculator** are the **Backspace** key that deletes the last number entered, the **MC** button that clears the **Calculator's** memory, and the **C** button that clears the current calculation.

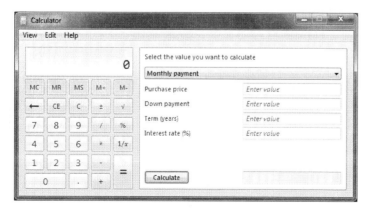

Figure 4-3: The Mortgage worksheet view in the Calculator window.

How to Work with the Calculator

Procedure Reference: Calculate Using the Calculator

To calculate using the **Calculator**:

1. Choose **Start→All Programs→Accessories→Calculator.**
2. On the **Calculator,** from the **View** menu, select an option to start calculating.
   - Choose **Standard** to perform a standard arithmetic calculation.
   - Choose **Scientific** to perform a logarithmic or trigonometric calculation.
   - Choose **Programmer** to perform a binary or decimal calculation.
   - Choose **Statistics** to perform a statistical calculation.
   - Select **History** to display the history of calculations and edit previous calculations.
   - Select **Digit grouping** to group the digits according to bases.
   - Select **Unit conversion** to convert from one unit of measurement to another.
   - Select **Date calculation** to calculate the difference between two given dates.
   - Select the corresponding **Worksheets** option to calculate mortgage payments, vehicle lease, and fuel economy rates.

Procedure Reference: Copy from the Calculator to WordPad

To copy from the **Calculator** to WordPad:

1. In the **Calculator** window, choose **Edit→Copy.**
2. In the **WordPad** window, paste the copied data in the desired location.

Procedure Reference: Paste Data in the Calculator

To paste data in the **Calculator**:

1. Copy numbers or data from any desired location.
2. In the **Calculator** window, choose **Edit→Paste.**

ACTIVITY 4-4
Using the Calculator with WordPad

Data Files:

My_letter to Smith homes.rtf

Before You Begin:

1. Navigate to the C:\084705Data folder, open the My_letter to Smith homes.rtf file in WordPad, and minimize the window.
2. Close Windows Explorer.

Scenario:

You are the property manager for Smith homes. A client is interested in buying a house at 18 Main St. The cost of the house is $127,300 and the down payment to be made is $31,500. You need to calculate the balance amount the client will need to mortgage. You also want to quote the calculated amount in a letter that is already drafted.

What You Do	How You Do It
1. Use the **Calculator** to calculate the mortgage amount.	a. Choose **Start→All Programs→Accessories→Calculator** to open the **Calculator** window.
	b. In the **Calculator** window, type *127300* to indicate the cost of the house.
	c. On the **Calculator,** click the **Minus** button.
	d. Type *31500* to indicate the down payment amount.
	e. On the **Calculator,** click the **Equal** button.
	f. Observe that the calculated balance is displayed as 95800.

2.	Copy the calculation into the WordPad document.	a.	In the **Calculator** window, choose **Edit→Copy**.
		b.	Minimize the **Calculator** window.
		c.	From the taskbar, restore the My_letter to Smith homes.rtf document.
		d.	In the **My_letter to Smith homes.rtf - WordPad** window, click the empty grid just below the **Need to Mortgage (in Dollars)** heading to position the cursor in that box.
		e.	On the Ribbon, on the **Home** tab, click the **Paste** button.
		f.	Similarly, calculate the mortgage amount for the houses on the other two streets and paste the answers in the second and third grids of the table in the My_letter to Smith homes.rtf file, respectively.
3.	Save and close the file.	a.	On the **Quick Access** toolbar, click the **Save** button.
		b.	Close the **My_letter to Smith homes.rtf - WordPad** and **Calculator** windows.

DISCOVERY ACTIVITY 4-5

Working with the Calculator

Scenario:
You need to prepare an expenses document. You decide to perform calculations using the **Calculator** application.

1. Which button will you press to clear the current calculation in the Calculator?
    a) The MR button
    b) The C button ✓
    c) The Backspace button
    d) The = button

2. Which button will you press to clear the Calculator's memory?
    a) The C button
    b) The MC button ✓
    c) The Backspace button
    d) The = button

TOPIC D
Customize a Graphic with the Paint Tool

You used the **Calculator** tool to perform calculations and copy them into WordPad. In addition to working with documents and numbers during common business tasks, you might need to work with graphic elements as well. There is another application in Windows 7 that allows you to edit pictures according to your requirements. In this topic, you will use the **Paint** tool to edit a picture and copy it into WordPad.

You may not have to deal with documents and textual content all the time; there may be times when you need to work with pictures and images. Being familiar with a graphic editing tool can come in handy when you need to do some basic image editing. Windows 7 provides you with the **Paint** tool, which has a variety of options that enable you to perform basic graphic editing tasks easily.

The Paint Tool

The *Paint tool* is a graphics program that provides a variety of options for creating and modifying pictures and images. Using this tool, you can not only draw and paint, but also edit images and add text to a picture. The title bar of the **Paint** window displays the **Quick Access** toolbar that allows you to access the commonly used commands. The Ribbon at the top of the **Paint** window contains a selection of commands that you may need to work on a graphic.

You can click the **Paint** button displayed at the top-left corner of the **Paint** window to perform file-related tasks such as printing and saving. The **Home** and **View** tabs are enclosed in a ribbon that displays commands and image viewing options in related groups. You can use the improved toolbar options such as brushes, zoom, ruler and gridlines, and full-screen mode to create better looking documents.

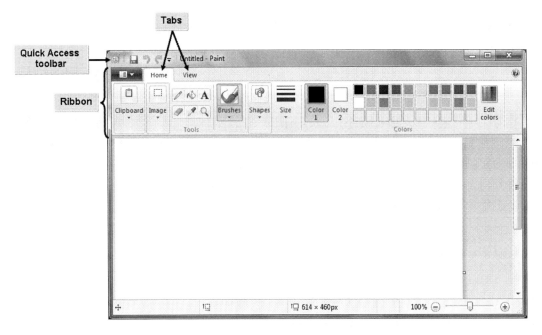

Figure 4-4: The Paint tool in Windows 7.

How to Customize a Graphic with the Paint Tool

Procedure Reference: Modify a Picture Using the Paint Tool

To modify a picture using the **Paint** tool:

1. Choose **Start→All Programs→Accessories→Paint.**
2. Display the **Open** dialog box.
   - In the **Paint** window, click the **Paint** button and from the drop-down menu, choose **Open.**
   - Or, press **Ctrl+O.**
3. Navigate to the desired location, select the image you want to modify, and click **Open.**
4. Modify the image using the options on the Ribbon.
   - Edit using the **Home** tab.
     - In the **Image** group, resize, flip, or crop the image to make a shaped selection.
     - In the **Tools** group, select the desired option to add text, color, or a drawing to the image. If necessary, select the **Eraser** or **Magnifier** tool to erase a part of the image and magnify the image, respectively.
     - In the **Brushes** group, select a brush with which you want to paint.
     - In the **Shapes** group, select a shape you want to insert in the **Paint** window. From the **Shape outline** and **Shape fill** drop-down lists, select the desired effects for the inserted shape.
     - In the **Size** group, select the desired size and thickness for the shape outline.
     - In the **Colors** section, select the desired color with which you want to paint. If necessary, click **Edit Colors** to display the **Edit Colors** dialog box from which you can select or customize colors.
   - Edit using the **View** tab.
     - In the **Zoom** group, select the desired option to change the zoom level of the image.
     - In the **Show or hide** group, select the components that you want to display in the **Paint** window.
     - In the **Display** group, select the view in which you want to view the image.

Procedure Reference: Add Text to a Picture in Paint

To add text to a picture in Paint:

1. Display the desired image in the **Paint** window.
2. On the Ribbon, on the **Home** tab, in the **Tools** group, select the **Text** tool.
3. On the **Canvas,** drag a text box using the I shaped pointer and type the desired text in the text box.
4. If necessary, format the text.
   - In the **Font** group, from the **Font family** drop-down list, select the desired font and from the **Font size** drop-down list, select the desired font size.
   - In the **Background** group, select the desired option to make the text look transparent or opaque.
   - In the **Colors** group, select a color that you want to apply to the entered text.

5. Save the picture.
   - Click the **Paint** button and choose **Save.**
   - On the **Quick Access** toolbar, click the **Save** button.
   - Or, press **Ctrl+S.**

 You can use the **Save as** option on the **Paint** menu if you want to save the modified image with a different name, in a different file format, or in a different location.

Procedure Reference: Copy a Picture from Paint to a WordPad Document

To copy a picture from Paint to a WordPad document:

1. Open the desired picture in Paint.
2. Using the desired selection option from the **Image** group, select the image.
3. Copy the selection.
   - In the **Clipboard** group, click **Copy.**
   - Right-click the selection and choose **Copy.**
   - Or, press **Ctrl+C.**
4. Open the WordPad document into which you want to paste the picture.
5. Place the insertion point in the desired position.
6. Paste the picture.
7. Save and close the document.

ACTIVITY 4-6
Using Paint with WordPad

Data Files:

Logo.jpg, My_letter to Smith homes.rtf

Before You Begin:

1. Navigate to the C:\084705Data folder, open the My_letter to Smith homes.rtf file in WordPad, and minimize the WordPad window.
2. Close Windows Explorer.

Scenario:

You have drafted an official letter in WordPad. You want to add your company logo at the bottom, below your signature. When you look at the logo, you realize that it does not have the company name on it. So, you decide to add the company name before inserting the logo into your letter.

What You Do	How You Do It
1. Open the picture to be edited.	a. Choose **Start→All Programs→Accessories→Paint**.
	b. If necessary, maximize the **Paint** window.
	c. Click the **Paint** button and choose **Open**.
	d. If necessary, navigate to the C:\084705Data folder, select and open the Logo.JPG file.

2. Edit the picture.

    a. In the **Tools** group, click the **Text** tool.

    b. In the space below the logo, click and drag the mouse pointer to draw a text box that covers the whole area under the logo.

    c. In the **Colors** group, in the second row, select the second color from the right.

    d. In the text box, type *Tri-Mark Properties*

    e. Click before the word "Tri," hold down **Shift,** and click after the word "Properties" to select the typed text.

    f. On the **Text** tab, in the **Font** group, from the **Font family** drop-down list, select **Georgia.**

    g. From the **Font size** drop-down list, select **12.**

    h. Click the **Paint** button and choose **Save as→PNG picture.**

    i. If necessary, in the **Save As** dialog box, navigate to the C:\084705Data folder.

    j. In the **File name** text box, type *My_logo*

    k. Click **Save.**

3. Copy and paste the picture into the WordPad document.

    a. In the **My_logo.png - Paint** window, on the **Home** tab, in the **Image** group, click the **Select** drop-down arrow and choose **Select all.**

    b. In the **Clipboard** group, click the **Copy** button.

    c. On the taskbar, click the **WordPad** icon to maximize the application.

    d. In the document area, click at the end of the text "Property Manager" and press **Enter.**

    e. In the **Clipboard** group, click the **Paste** button to paste the image in WordPad.

    f. On the **Quick Access** toolbar, click the **Save** button.

    g. Close the **WordPad** and **Paint** windows.

DISCOVERY ACTIVITY 4-7
Working with Paint

Scenario:
You are the owner of an IT company and you have hired a graphic designer to make some modifications to your existing company logo. You want to give him a set of requirements as to what changes you want in the logo along with a sample.

1. Which group in the Paint window contains the Text tool?
    a) Clipboard
    b) Shapes
    c) Image
    d) Tools ✓

2. True or False? You can adjust the size and thickness of a shape inserted in the Paint window.
    X True
    ___ False

Lesson 4 Follow-up

In this lesson, you worked with some of the common applications that are built into Windows 7 such as WordPad, Paint, and Calculator. By using these basic sets of applications, you can perform some simple tasks, such as drafting letters, calculating and solving math problems, editing pictures effectively and efficiently without having to purchase additional software.

1. **What are the different situations that may require you to use the Paint application?**

2. **How useful is the WordPad application to you in your work?**

5 | Customizing the Windows 7 Desktop

Lesson Time: 1 hour(s), 10 minutes

Lesson Objectives:

In this lesson, you will customize the Windows 7 desktop using the customizing tools and shortcuts to personalize the desktop to suit your business requirements.

You will:

- Customize the Start menu using the Start Menu Properties dialog box to match a desired configuration.

- Customize the taskbar to add programs and notifications to access programs and tools directly from the taskbar.

- Personalize the desktop using the Personalization menu to apply a personalized setting to the desktop.

- Set a screen saver using the Personalization menu to activate the screen saver when the computer is idle for a long time.

- Add gadgets to the desktop using the desktop Gadgets gallery to display gadget-specific information.

Introduction

You used applications to create documents and save them as files on your hard disk. You can customize all the desktop elements to suit your work needs. In this lesson, you will customize the various elements on your desktop.

At the office, some people may like to decorate their cubicles with objects of their choice to add life and color to their surroundings. One of the best things about Windows 7 is the ability to customize nearly every element on the screen—the desktop icons, fonts, colors, pictures, and window styles that make it all the more interesting to work with.

TOPIC A
Customize the Start Menu

You are familiar with the **Start** menu and its features. You can use the **Start** menu more efficiently by placing the frequently accessed programs in the program list and by adjusting other properties. In this topic, you will customize the **Start** menu.

Before you start your day at the office, you want to ensure that you have all the resources and tools available to facilitate your job. Similarly, customizing the **Start** menu will help you easily access frequently used programs that you may need to use during the day.

The Start Menu Properties Dialog Box

The **Start** menu properties determine the way links, icons, and menus look and behave on the **Start** menu of a computer. You can customize these properties on the **Start Menu** tab of the **Taskbar and Start Menu Properties** dialog box. This dialog box allows you to select programs and specify the number of recent items you want to view on the **Start** menu and also in the Jump Lists.

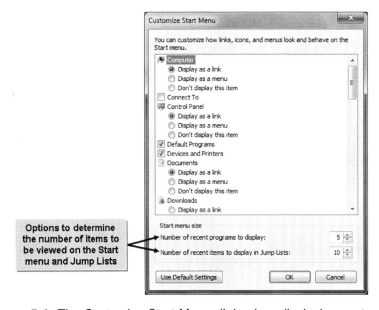

Figure 5-1: The Customize Start Menu dialog box displaying customizing options.

How to Customize the Start Menu

Procedure Reference: Add a Program to the Start Menu

To add a program to the **Start** menu:
1. On the **Start** menu, locate the program you want to add to the **Start** menu.
2. Right-click the program icon and choose **Pin to Start Menu.**

Procedure Reference: Remove a Program from the Start Menu

To remove a program from the **Start** menu:
1. On the **Start** menu, choose the program you want to remove.
2. Remove the program.
   - Right-click the program icon and choose **Unpin from Start Menu.**
   - Or, right-click the program icon and choose **Remove from this list.**

Procedure Reference: Customize the Start Menu Properties

To customize the default **Start** menu properties:
1. Right-click the **Start** button and choose **Properties** to open the **Taskbar and Start Menu Properties** dialog box.
2. Customize the **Start** menu properties.
   - Click **Customize** to open the **Customize Start Menu** dialog box and modify the properties.
     - Select the options that you want to display as shortcuts or menu items on the **Start** menu.
     - In the **Start menu size** section, in the **Number of recent programs to display** spin box, specify the number of recent programs that you want the **Start** menu to display.
     - In the **Number of recent items to display in Jump Lists** spin box, specify the number of recent items that you want the Jump Lists to display.
     - Click **OK** to apply the modified settings and to close the **Customize Start Menu** dialog box.
     - If necessary, click **Use Default Settings** to use the Windows 7 default **Start** menu properties.
   - In the **Taskbar and Start Menu Properties** dialog box, from the **Power button action** drop-down list, select the function that you want the power button to perform.
   - In the **Privacy** section, check the desired check boxes to specify the privacy settings of the **Start** menu.
3. Click **OK** to close the **Taskbar and Start Menu Properties** dialog box.

Introduction to Personal Computers Using Windows® 7

ACTIVITY 5-1
Customizing the Start Menu

Before You Begin:
The Windows 7 desktop is displayed.

Scenario:
Next week, you will be attending an international seminar as a part of World Conservation Day. You will be using **Notepad** to make notes during the session. To quickly access Notepad, you decide to pin the Notepad program icon to your **Start** menu. You also want to limit the number of programs displayed in the frequently accessed programs section to ensure that your **Start** menu is not cluttered. In addition, you will be using the printer frequently. So, you want to have the **Printers** icon displayed in the right pane of the **Start** menu.

What You Do	How You Do It
1. Pin the **Notepad** icon to the **Start** menu.	a. Choose **Start→All Programs→Accessories**.
	b. On the **Accessories** submenu, right-click the **Notepad** icon and choose **Pin to Start Menu**.
	c. Hover the mouse pointer over **Back** to return to the default programs list on the **Start** menu.
	d. Observe that the **Notepad** icon is added to the pinned items list of the **Start** menu.
2. Limit the number of programs displayed in the frequently accessed programs list.	a. Right-click the **Start** button and choose **Properties**.
	b. In the **Taskbar and Start Menu Properties** dialog box, on the **Start Menu** tab, click **Customize**.
	c. In the **Customize Start Menu** dialog box, in the **Start menu size** section, in the **Number of recent programs to display** spin box, double-click and type **5**

Lesson 5: Customizing the Windows 7 Desktop

3.	Display the **Devices and Printers** icon on the **Start** menu.	a.	In the displayed list, observe that the **Devices and Printers** check box is checked.
		b.	Click **OK** to close the **Customize Start Menu** dialog box.
		c.	In the **Taskbar and Start Menu Properties** dialog box, click **Apply** and then click **OK** to apply the modified settings.
4.	Observe the customized **Start** menu.	a.	Click the **Start** button.
		b.	Observe that the number of programs in the **Start** menu default programs list is five and the **Notepad** icon that was pinned to the **Start** menu is located besides the programs that were added in the **Start menu size** section.
		c.	Observe that the **Devices and Printers** link appears in the right pane of the **Start** menu.
		d.	Click the **Start** button again to close the **Start** menu.

DISCOVERY ACTIVITY 5-2
Organizing the Start Menu

Scenario:
Prior to a meeting at your client's workplace, you want to ensure that you have pinned all the programs you frequently use to the **Start** menu.

1. Which option on the Start menu enables you to add programs to it so that you can access the added programs quickly and easily?

    a) Add to Start Menu

    (b) Pin to Start Menu

    c) Default Programs

    d) Properties

2. True or False? The Pin to Start Menu option enables you to add a program icon to the frequently used program section of the Start menu.

    ___ True

    _X_ False

TOPIC B
Customize the Taskbar

You are now familiar with how to customize the **Start** menu. The taskbar is another desktop item that, when customized, can help you quickly launch new program windows or manage existing ones with ease. In this topic, you will customize the taskbar.

Many people enjoy playing music on the computer while working; however, it can be tedious to navigate through the menus to launch the music player application. It might be easier if you could launch the program with just a click. Customizing the taskbar helps you arrange your favorite program icons so that you can access them with a single click right from the desktop.

How to Customize the Taskbar
Procedure Reference: Customize the Taskbar

To customize the taskbar:

1. Right-click the taskbar and choose **Properties** to open the **Taskbar and Start Menu Properties** dialog box.
2. Customize the taskbar.
   - In the **Taskbar appearance** section, make the desired settings.
     - Check the **Lock the taskbar** check box to ensure that the position of the taskbar is fixed in the desired location.
     - Check the **Auto-hide the taskbar** check box to ensure that the taskbar is always hidden and appears only when you point to it.
     - Check the **Use small icons** check box to decrease the size of the taskbar icons.
     - From the **Taskbar location on screen** drop-down list, select the desired location for the taskbar.
     - From the **Taskbar buttons** drop-down list, select the desired grouping pattern for the taskbar icons.
   - In the **Preview desktop with Aero Peek** section, check the **Use Aero Peek to preview the desktop** check box to activate the Aero Peek feature.
   - In the **Notification area** section, click **Customize** to customize the notification area of the taskbar.
     - In the **Select which icons and notifications appear on the taskbar** section, from the **Behaviors** drop-down list, select the desired option to show or hide notifications.
     - Check the **Always show all icons and notifications on the taskbar** check box to display all the icons and notifications.
     - Click the **Turn system icons on or off** link to display the **Turn system icons on or off** section and from the **Behaviors** drop-down list, select the desired option to turn a system icon on or off and click **OK.**
     - In the **Select which icons and notifications appear on the taskbar** section, click the **Restore default icon behaviors** link to restore the Windows 7 default icon behaviors and click **OK.**
   - Add toolbars to the taskbar.

a. Select the **Toolbars** tab.
b. In the **Select which toolbars to add to the taskbar** section, check the desired check boxes.
3. Click **Apply** to apply the changes.
4. Click **OK** to close the **Taskbar and Start Menu Properties** dialog box.

Customizing the Notification Icons

You can also customize the notification icons on the taskbar by right-clicking the notification area and choosing **Customize notification icons** or by clicking the **Show hidden icons** arrow button on the left of the taskbar and clicking the **Customize** link.

Adding Toolbars to the Taskbar

You can also add toolbars to the taskbar by right-clicking the taskbar and choosing the desired toolbar from the **Toolbars** submenu.

Procedure Reference: Pin an Item to the Taskbar

To pin an item to the taskbar:
1. Right-click the desired program on the **Start** menu or the taskbar.
2. Pin the program to the taskbar.
   - On the right-click menu of the program on the **Start** menu, choose **Pin to Taskbar**.
   - On the right-click menu of the program on the taskbar, choose **Pin this program to taskbar.**

Pinning and Reordering Programs on the Taskbar

You can open a file in another program and pin the file to the relevant icon of that program on the taskbar to always open the file in that program. For example, you can open a .txt file in WordPad and pin that file to the **WordPad** icon on the taskbar to always open the file in WordPad. You can also drag items from any other location to pin them to the taskbar. Icons of the taskbar can be clicked and dragged to reorder them to a different location on the taskbar.

Color Effect on Taskbar Icons

When you are working with several open windows, the program icon on the taskbar displays a glossy light effect indicating the open program.

Procedure Reference: Change the Location of the Taskbar

To change the location of the taskbar:
1. If necessary, unlock the taskbar by unchecking the **Lock the taskbar** check box on the context menu of the taskbar or in the **Taskbar and Start Menu Properties** dialog box.
2. Click the taskbar and drag it to any one of the four sides of your screen to position it in the desired location.

Changing the Location of the Taskbar

You can also change the position of the taskbar on the **Taskbar** tab of the **Taskbar and Start Menu Properties** dialog box by selecting the desired option from the **Taskbar location on screen** drop-down list.

ACTIVITY 5-3
Customizing the Taskbar

Before You Begin:
The Windows 7 desktop is displayed with the taskbar.

Scenario:
You are assigned a high priority project that has to be completed in a very short span of time. To save time and avoid the trouble of accessing each and every program from its original location, you want to pin the programs to your taskbar. To make things more simpler, you also want to have the windows of the same program grouped together, hide the less frequently used icons in the **Notification** area of the taskbar, and display the items that can be accessed from the desktop to be displayed in the form of a menu.

What You Do	How You Do It
1. Observe the default taskbar settings.	a. Right-click the taskbar and choose **Properties** to open the **Taskbar and Start Menu Properties** dialog box.
	b. In the **Taskbar appearance** section, observe that the **Lock the taskbar** check box is checked and in the **Taskbar buttons** drop-down list, the **Always combine, hide labels** option is selected.

Introduction to Personal Computers Using Windows® 7

2. Customize the taskbar to control the display of icons in the **Notification** area.

   a. On the taskbar, in the **Notification** area, observe that the **Action Center, Network,** and **Volume** icons are displayed.

   b. In the **Taskbar and Start Menu Properties** dialog box, in the **Notification area** section, click **Customize** to access the **Notification Area Icons** window.

   c. In the **Notification Area Icons** window, in the **Behaviors** column, from the drop-down list to the right of the **Network** column, select **Hide icon and notifications** to hide the **Network** icon and its corresponding notifications.

   d. Similarly, hide the **Volume** icon and its corresponding notifications.

   e. Click **OK** to apply the settings.

   f. Observe that the **Network** and **Volume** icons are no longer displayed in the **Notification** area of the taskbar.

3. Add a new toolbar to the taskbar.

   a. If necessary, display the **Taskbar and Start Menu Properties** dialog box.

   b. In the **Taskbar and Start Menu Properties** dialog box, select the **Toolbars** tab.

   c. In the **Select which toolbars to add to the taskbar** section, check the **Desktop** check box.

   d. Click **Apply** to apply the settings.

   e. Click **OK** to close the **Taskbar and Start Menu Properties** dialog box.

   f. Observe that a new **Desktop** toolbar with a dual arrow is added to the taskbar.

   g. On the **Desktop** toolbar, click the dual arrows to view the list of programs that you can access from the desktop.

   h. Click the dual arrows again to close the **Desktop** menu.

Lesson 5: Customizing the Windows 7 Desktop

4.	Pin the **WordPad** program icon to the taskbar.	a.	Choose **Start→All Programs→Accessories.**
		b.	On the **Accessories** submenu, right-click the **WordPad** icon and choose **Pin to Taskbar.**
		c.	Observe that the **WordPad** icon appears on the taskbar from where you can access the program quickly.
		d.	Click the **Start** button again to close the **Start** menu.
5.	Customize the display of the taskbar.	a.	On the taskbar, right-click and uncheck the **Lock the Taskbar** option.
		b.	Click the center of the taskbar and drag it to the left of the desktop.
		c.	On the taskbar, right-click and choose **Properties.**
		d.	In the **Taskbar and Start Menu Properties** dialog box, in the **Taskbar appearance** section, check the **Auto-hide the taskbar** check box and click **OK** to hide the taskbar.
		e.	Place the mouse pointer at the left edge of the screen to display the taskbar.
		f.	On the taskbar, right-click and choose **Properties.**
		g.	If necessary, move the **Taskbar and Start Menu Properties** dialog box away from the taskbar.
		h.	In the **Taskbar appearance** section, uncheck the **Auto-hide the taskbar** check box and click **OK** to display the taskbar.
		i.	Click the center of the taskbar and drag it to the bottom of the desktop.

Introduction to Personal Computers Using Windows® 7

DISCOVERY ACTIVITY 5-4
Organizing the Taskbar

Scenario:
You are a net-savvy person who spends hours blogging. To ensure that you spend your time productively, you decide to customize the taskbar to help manage your workflow.

1. **Which option in the Taskbar and Start Menu Properties dialog box hides the taskbar automatically when not in use?**

    a) Lock the taskbar

    b) Auto-hide the taskbar ✓

    c) Taskbar buttons

    d) Taskbar location on screen

2. **Identify the options in the Taskbar and Start Menu Properties dialog box for customizing the taskbar.**

    a) Taskbar buttons ✓

    b) Notification area ✓

    c) Preview desktop with Aero Peek ✓

    d) Task Manager

TOPIC C
Personalize the Desktop

You have customized the **Start** menu and the taskbar. You can also customize the desktop with many options to make your Windows 7 work environment appealing and useful. In this topic, you will personalize your desktop.

Because the desktop is the work area where dialog boxes, windows, icons, and menus appear, and essentially the location where all of your work takes place, it makes sense to make the desktop aesthetically appealing. Windows 7 enables you to modify the desktop to suit your tastes and needs.

Personalization Options

You can personalize the settings on your computer using the options in the **Personalization** window.

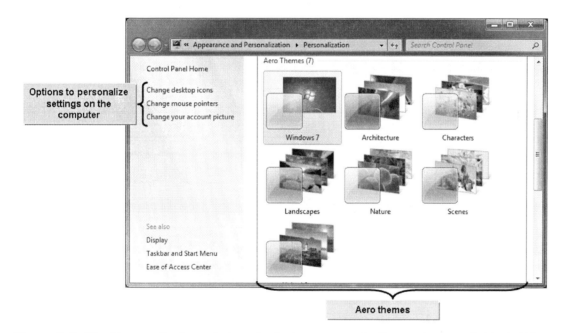

Figure 5-2: The Personalization window displaying personalization options available in Windows 7.

The options in the **Personalization** window are described in the following table.

Personalization Option	Description
Change desktop icons	Enables you to select the icons you want to display on your desktop and also change the display image of the icons.

Personalization Option	Description
Change mouse pointers	Enables you to customize the behavior of mouse pointers for mouse actions such as selecting text, resizing and moving windows, hovering over links, and so on.
Change your account picture	Enables you to choose a new picture for your account, which is displayed on the **Start** menu and **Welcome** screen.
Aero Themes	Enables you to apply an Aero theme that enhances the taskbar and display the functionality of the desktop.
Basic and High Contrast Themes	Enables you to apply a basic Windows theme to the desktop.
Desktop Background	Enables you to choose a picture to make it your desktop background or select multiple pictures and time them to create a desktop slide show.
Window Color	Enables you to customize the appearance of your windows, the **Start** menu, and taskbar by adjusting their color and style.
Sounds	Enables you to choose sound schemes and specify settings for audio files to play for various system events such as the arrival of a new mail message or a system notification.
Screen Saver	Enables you to choose from a list of screen savers or adjust the screen saver settings.

The Desktop Background

The *desktop background,* also known as wallpaper, is a picture that you can display on your desktop. You can choose to fit the picture to the entire screen, stretch it across your desktop, display it in a tiled fashion, or center it on your desktop. If you want a picture on a web page to be set as your desktop background, you can right-click the image and choose **Set as Background.** You can also create a desktop slide show by selecting multiple desktop backgrounds and specifying time for the change of pictures.

How to Personalize the Desktop

Procedure Reference: Change the Desktop Background

To change the desktop background:

1. Right-click the desktop and choose **Personalize** to display the **Personalization** window.
2. In the **Change the visuals and sounds on your computer** section, click **Desktop Background.**
3. In the **Choose your desktop background** section, from the **Picture location** drop-down list, select the location where the images are saved, or click **Browse** to locate the folder where the desired pictures are stored.
4. Select the image that you want to display as your desktop background or click **Select all** to select all the images to create a desktop slide show.
5. If necessary, specify the options to set the position of the image on the desktop or create a desktop slide show.
   - From the **Picture position** drop-down list, select the desired size of the image you want to display on the desktop.
   - From the **Change picture every** drop-down list, select the time gap for changing the pictures for a desktop slide show.
   - Click **Shuffle** to change the order of the images for a desktop slide show.
   - Click **Clear all** to deselect the selected images or to make a new selection.
6. Click **Save changes** to apply the changes to the desktop background.
7. If necessary, minimize the **Personalization** window to view the new desktop background.

Applying Solid Colors as Desktop Backgrounds

You can select and apply a solid color as your desktop background instead of an image. In the **Personalization** window, in the **choose your desktop background** section, in the **Picture location** drop-down list, the **Solid Colors** option is available by default. You can click **More** to display the **Color** dialog box and select from a wide range of basic colors and customize colors and apply them as your desktop background.

Procedure Reference: Add or Remove Common Desktop Icons

To add or remove common desktop icons:

1. Display the **Personalization** window.
2. In the left pane, click the **Change desktop icons** link to display the **Desktop Icon Settings** dialog box.
3. In the **Desktop Icon Settings** dialog box, in the **Desktop Icons** section, check or uncheck the check boxes for the icons that you want to add or remove from your desktop.
4. If necessary, specify other options to change the desktop icon settings in Windows 7.
   - Click **Change Icon** to display the **Change Icon** dialog box, select a different display image for the desired icon and click **OK.**
   - Check the **Allow themes to change desktop icons** check box to allow the themes to modify the desktop icons.
   - Click **Restore Default** to restore the default desktop icon settings.
5. Click **OK** to close the **Desktop Icon Settings** dialog box.
6. Close the **Personalization** window.

Procedure Reference: Arrange Desktop Icons

To arrange desktop icons:

1. Right-click an empty location on your desktop.
2. From the displayed menu, choose **Sort by** and then choose an option to sort the icons on the desktop.
   - Choose **Name** to arrange icons in alphabetical order.
   - Choose **Size** to arrange icons in an increasing order of the object size.
   - Choose **Item type** to group similar icons together.
   - Choose **Date modified** to group icons in a chronological order of their modification.

ACTIVITY 5-5
Personalizing the Desktop

Before You Begin:
The Windows 7 desktop is displayed.

Scenario:
You want to add a personal touch to your desktop so that you may find it interesting to work on it everyday. So, you decide to enhance your desktop by applying a scenic picture of a rolling meadow. You also want to try out certain simple backgrounds such as solid colors. Because you will be making constant changes to the settings on your computer and accessing the network frequently, you decide to add the **Network** and **Control Panel** icons to your desktop.

What You Do	How You Do It
1. Set a picture as your desktop background.	a. Right-click the desktop and choose **Personalize** to display the **Personalization** window.
	b. If necessary, maximize the **Personalization** window.
	c. On the **Change the visuals and sounds on your computer** page, click **Desktop Background**.
	d. On the **Choose your desktop background** page, in the **Picture location** drop-down list, observe that the **Windows Desktop Backgrounds** location is selected.
	e. In the **United States** section, select the fourth image from the left.
	f. Click **Save changes** and close the **Personalization** window.
	g. Observe that the selected image is applied as your desktop background.
	h. Right-click the desktop and choose **Personalize**.
	i. In the **Personalization** window, click **Desktop Background**.
	j. On the **Choose your desktop background** page, from the **Picture location** drop-down list, select **Solid Colors**.
	k. From the color box displayed, in the first row, select the third blue color from the right.
	l. Click **Save changes** and close the **Personalization** window to view the color change.

2. Display the **Control Panel** and **Network** icons on your desktop.

   a. Right-click the desktop and choose **Personalize**.

   b. In the **Personalization** window, in the left pane, click **Change desktop icons**.

   c. In the **Desktop Icon Settings** dialog box, check the **Control Panel** and **Network** check boxes.

   d. Click **Apply** to apply the changes.

   e. Click **OK** to close the **Desktop Icon Settings** dialog box.

   f. Close the **Personalization** window.

   g. Observe that the **Control Panel** and **Network** icons are added to your desktop.

DISCOVERY ACTIVITY 5-6
Working with Windows 7 Desktop Elements

Scenario:
You have just purchased a new personal computer with Windows 7 installed on it and you want your desktop to have a refreshing look. You decide to test the different personalization options available and apply a few options to your desktop.

1. **Which option will you choose from the desktop right-click menu to arrange icons in alphabetical order?**

    ⓐ) Sort by→Name.

    b) Sort by→Size.

    c) Sort by→Item type.

    d) Sort by→Date modified.

2. **True or False? It is possible to specify a color for your desktop background instead of an image.**

    ✗ True

    __ False

TOPIC D
Set a Screen Saver

You have set the desktop wallpaper. At times when the computer is not in use, you can set a screen saver to hide your work. In this topic, you will set a screen saver.

You may have to leave your computer temporarily while you work. It is not practical to log off your computer every time you leave for a short time because it takes too long to resume your work. A screen saver can come in handy during these times by displaying an animation on your desktop. This prevents people passing by from seeing what is on your screen and also locks your system automatically to protect it.

Screen Savers
Definition:

A *screen saver* is a slide show of a picture or text that is displayed automatically on a computer screen when the computer is idle for a set period of time. You can define the settings for the screen saver, such as the idle time that prompts the slide show, the text to be displayed, the font, and other properties of a text animation. You can also select the surface style of the screen saver and modify its display settings.

Example:

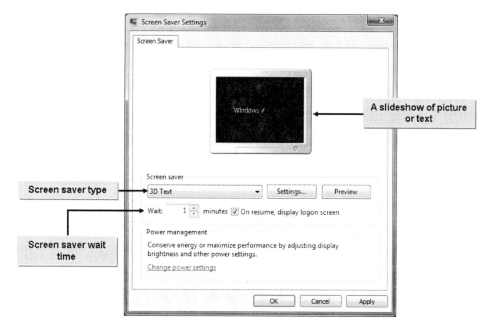

Figure 5-3: The Screen Saver Settings dialog box displaying screen saving options in Windows 7.

Purpose of Screen Savers

In the past, screen savers were used to prevent screen burns. If a computer was left on for a long time, the open window's image would be burned into the screen so that a ghostly image of the window would remain on the screen, even if the window was no longer open. Though once common, screen burn is not very common any more. In general, screen savers are primarily deployed to prevent people passing by from seeing what is on your screen.

How to Set a Screen Saver

Procedure Reference: Set a Screen Saver

To set a screen saver:

1. Display the **Personalization** window.
2. In the **Change the visuals and sounds on your computer** section, click **Screen Saver.**
3. In the **Screen Saver Settings** dialog box, from the **Screen saver** drop-down list, select the desired screen saver.
4. If necessary, specify the other screen saver settings.
    - Click **Settings** and modify the text, motion, resolution, display, and surface style settings as desired.
    - In the **Wait** spin box, specify the number of minutes you want the screen saver to be displayed on the desktop.
    - Check the **On resume, display logon screen** check box to display the logon screen after the screen saver is displayed for the specified period of time.
    - Click **Preview** to preview the screen saver before applying it.
5. Click **Apply** to apply the screen saver settings.
6. Click **OK** to close the **Screen Saver Settings** dialog box.
7. Close the **Personalization** window.

ACTIVITY 5-7
Setting a Screen Saver

Before You Begin:
The Windows 7 desktop is displayed.

Scenario:
You are working on an assignment that requires you to print many documents. Because you need to go to the printer frequently to collect the printouts, you decide to set a screen saver to prevent people passing by your desk from viewing confidential documents.

What You Do	How You Do It
1. Select a screen saver.	a. Right-click the desktop and choose **Personalize**.
	b. In the **Personalization** window, on the **Change the visuals and sounds on your computer** page, click **Screen Saver**.
	c. In the **Screen Saver Settings** dialog box, from the **Screen saver** drop-down list, select **3D Text**.

2. Configure the screen saver settings.

   a. In the **Wait** text box, double-click the existing value and type *2* to set the delay time as two minutes.

   b. In the **Screen saver** section, click **Settings.**

   c. In the **3D Text Settings** dialog box, in the **Motion** section, from the **Rotation Type** drop-down list, select **None** and click **OK.**

   d. In the **Screen Saver Settings** dialog box, click **Preview** to preview the screen saver.

   e. On the keyboard, press any key to exit from the screen saver preview.

   f. In the **Screen Saver Settings** dialog box, click **Apply** to apply the settings.

   g. Click **OK** to close the **Screen Saver Settings** dialog box.

   h. Close the **Personalization** window.

DISCOVERY ACTIVITY 5-8
Examining Screen Saver Settings Options

Scenario:
You are the Human Resources manager of an organization. You are working on an important presentation, which you do not want your colleagues to know about. Because you have to move away from your desk for a few minutes and you do not want to close the presentation, you decide to apply a screen saver. You examine the screen saver options available to you.

1. **What does the Wait option in the Screen Saver Settings dialog box denote?**

    ⓐ) The idle time after which the screen saver gets activated.

    b) The time for which the screen saver is displayed.

    c) The time interval between two screen saver sessions.

    d) The time after which the next screen saver option is activated.

2. **True or False? Screen savers are primarily used to prevent people passing by from seeing what is on your computer screen.**

    ☒ True

    ___ False

TOPIC E
Add Gadgets

You customized and personalized the desktop. There are certain customizing techniques whose results can be dynamic. In this topic, you will work with the Windows 7 gadgets to display various types of dynamic content on the desktop.

Assume that you are a business executive and your job role requires you to travel frequently. Sometimes, you may need a quick update on weather reports or news headlines, but you may not have the time to browse a website to check for updates. Additionally, it will be very helpful if you could quickly check your appointments in the calendar. Being able to access information directly from your desktop will help you save time and effort. Windows 7 provides you with various gadgets that help you handle tasks easily and swiftly.

Gadgets

Definition:

A *gadget* is a mini application that is programmed to provide specific information at a glance. It can be configured to appear anywhere on the desktop. A gadget may have additional options to change its display style. There are free gadgets that can be downloaded from the Internet and can be added to the **Gadgets** gallery.

Example:

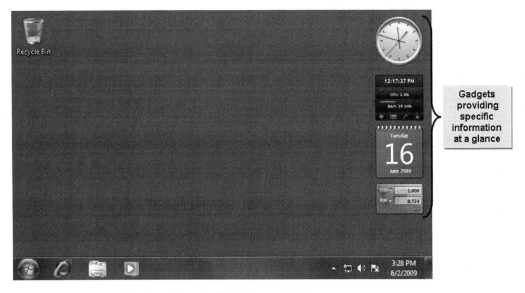

Figure 5-4: Gadgets displayed on the Windows 7 desktop.

The Gadgets Gallery

The *Gadgets gallery* displays the list of default gadgets available in Windows 7 and enables you to download different types of gadgets.

The gadgets available in the **Gadgets** gallery are described in the following table.

Gadget	Description
Calendar	Displays calendar information such as date, day, month, and year. You can also view the calendar for the entire month.
Clock	Displays the time for the selected time zone.
CPU Meter	Displays the CPU and RAM usage of your computer.
Currency	Displays the currency conversion rates for currencies of different countries.
Feed Headlines	Displays the RSS feeds from websites. RSS feed is a feature that allows you to receive regular updates on news events or specific areas of interest from the Internet.
Picture Puzzle	Displays a picture puzzle and also provides additional picture puzzles to solve.
Slide Show	Displays a slide show of pictures from a selected folder.
Stocks	Displays the stock information of various stock markets around the world.
Weather	Displays weather information such as temperature and weather forecasts for the next three days.
Windows Media Center	Displays the latest TV recordings, Internet TV clips, your favorite pictures, and music files.

How to Add Gadgets

Procedure Reference: Display a Gadget on the Desktop

To display a gadget on the desktop:

1. Right-click the desktop and choose **Gadgets** to display the **Gadgets** gallery.
2. Select the desired gadget.
3. If necessary, at the bottom of the **Gadgets** gallery, click **Show details** to view more details about the selected gadget.
4. Display the gadget on your desktop.
   - Right-click the selected gadget and choose **Add.**
   - Drag the gadget to the desired location on the desktop.
   - Or, double-click the gadget.
5. Close the **Gadgets** gallery.

Procedure Reference: Modify the Gadget Options

To modify the gadget options:

1. Display the desired gadget on the desktop.
2. Change the settings of the gadget.
   - Right-click the gadget and from the **Size** submenu, choose the desired option or click the **Larger size/Smaller size** button to change the size of the gadget.
   - Right-click the gadget and choose **Move** to display the four-headed arrow and click anywhere on the desktop to change the location of the gadget. Or, select the gadget and drag it using the **Drag gadget** button.
   - Right-click the gadget and choose **Options** to change the types and time zones of the gadget.
   - Right-click the gadget and choose **Always on top** to display the gadget on top of every window you open.
   - Right-click the gadget and from the **Opacity** submenu, choose the desired opacity level to make the gadget look transparent.
   - Right-click the gadget and choose **Add gadgets** to display the **Gadgets** gallery to add more gadgets.

Procedure Reference: Detach a Gadget

To detach a gadget:

1. Select the gadget on the desktop.
2. Close the gadget.
   - Right-click the gadget and choose **Close gadget.**
   - Or, click the **Close** button located next to the gadget.

ACTIVITY 5-9
Adding Gadgets to the Desktop

Before You Begin:
The Windows 7 desktop is displayed.

Scenario:
You need to frequently organize and attend meetings, so you want a convenient way to check your calendar and time. You also want to keep a check on the latest currency values and conversion rates. You want to add gadgets to your desktop so that you can quickly view and access the needed information.

What You Do	How You Do It
1. Add gadgets to the desktop.	a. Right-click the desktop and choose **Gadgets** to display the **Gadgets** gallery.
	b. In the **Gadgets** gallery, observe that the **Calendar** gadget icon is selected and click **Show details** to view details about the gadget.
	c. Double-click the **Calendar** gadget icon to add it to the desktop.
	d. Observe that the **Calendar** gadget is added to the desktop.
	e. Similarly, add the **Currency** and **Clock** gadgets to the desktop.
	f. Close the **Gadgets** gallery.

2. Modify the **Clock** settings.

   a. Right-click the **Clock** gadget and choose **Options** to display the **Clock** dialog box.

   b. Below the displayed clock layout, click the **Next** button to change the clock layout.

   c. From the **Time zone** drop-down list, select **Pacific Time (US & Canada).**

   d. Check the **Show the second hand** check box.

   e. Click **OK.**

   f. Observe that the changes are reflected on the **Clock** gadget.

3. Remove the **Calendar** gadget from the desktop.

   a. Right-click the **Calendar** gadget and choose **Close gadget** to close the gadget.

   b. Observe that the **Calendar** gadget is no longer displayed on the desktop.

DISCOVERY ACTIVITY 5-10

Working with Windows 7 Gadgets

Scenario:
You want to add gadgets to your desktop to have a quick look at the date and time whenever needed during your work.

1. What are the default gadgets available in the Windows 7 Gadgets gallery?

    ⓐ) Clock

    b) Traffic Update

    ⓒ) Weather

    d) Feed Headlines

2. True or False? All the gadgets are provided with customization options.

    ~~True~~

    ☒ False

Lesson 5 Follow-up

In this lesson, you customized your Windows 7 desktop. You customized every element of the desktop such as the **Start** menu, taskbar, and background to suit your needs. Customizing the settings on your computer can help you create a personalized work environment for higher productivity and efficiency.

1. Which gadgets will you add to your desktop? Why?

2. Of all the customization tasks performed on desktop elements, which task did you find the most useful? Why?

6 Browsing the Internet

Lesson Time: 40 minutes

Lesson Objectives:

In this lesson, you will examine networking tools and features so that you can browse for information using the Internet.

You will:

- Define networks to identify the various network components.
- Browse websites using Internet Explorer 8 to view the content of the desired websites.

Introduction

You are now familiar with folder and file management in Windows 7. You have also customized your desktop to suit your work needs. In addition to using a computer to work with and manage data, another important use of it is to access and gather information from the Internet. In this lesson, you will use a web browser to browse the Internet.

The Internet enables you to obtain information on any topic, send and receive messages, listen to music, download utilities and gadgets, shop online, and keep in touch with others, no matter where you are located. Because the Internet is a ubiquitous and powerful tool for both personal and business needs, every computer user should be able to browse the Internet and use its resources effectively.

TOPIC A
An Overview of Networks

You have been exposed to managing files and folders and have customized your Windows 7 desktop. You should also realize the need to communicate over a network. Before communicating over the network, you need to understand computer networks and the basic network components. In this topic, you will identify a network and its various components.

With the evolution of e-commerce, online transactions, and home businesses, the Internet has become the preferred way of conducting business in any organization as well as to accomplish many personal tasks for individuals. From accessing the vast amounts of information on just about every known subject to mankind, to services such as online banking and online travel reservations, the Internet has become an indispensable part in day-to-day life. Windows 7 provides you with Internet Explorer 8, an interface to browse contents and access resources on the Internet. Developing your browsing skills will allow you to use the Internet effectively.

Computer Networks

Definition:

A *computer network* is a group of computers that are connected together to communicate and share resources such as files, printers, and email. Generally, a network is formed when two or more computers are connected through a cable, network adapter, network operating system, and network protocol to control communication. Networks can cover a small area, such as an office building, or span a large geographic area, such as a nation or the entire world. There are no limitations on the size of a network.

Example:

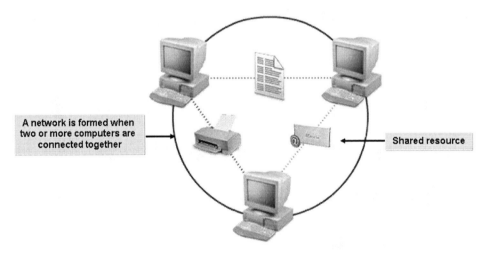

Figure 6-1: *A group of computers connected to the network.*

Network Uses

A computer network is used for two important reasons—communicating and sharing resources. While communicating enables you to exchange information easily, accessing shared network resources such as files, applications, or hardware, expands the capabilities of each computer on the network.

Types of Networks

There are different types of network models to choose from depending on your requirements. The following table provides a description of each of them.

Network Model	Description
Centralized	A *centralized network* is a network in which a central computer controls all network communication and performs data processing and storage on behalf of clients. Users connect to the host via dedicated terminals. The terminals have few or no local computing resources of their own. Centralized networks are also called "hierarchical networks" and "host-based networks."
Client-server	A *client-server network* is a network in which computer functionality is divided into two roles: *server* computers that provide services and control network operations and *client* computers that use services. Servers also provide access to shared files, printers, hardware, and applications.
Peer-to-peer	A *peer-to-peer network,* sometimes called a workgroup, is a network in which resource sharing, processing, and communication controls are completely decentralized. All clients on the network are equal in terms of providing and using resources. Peer-to-peer networks are easy and inexpensive to implement. However, they are only practical in very small organizations, due to the lack of central data storage and administration.

ACTIVITY 6-1
Identifying Basic Network Components

Scenario:
A network has been set up in your office. You want to understand the basic network components before you start using your office network.

1. What is a computer network?

    a) A set of hardware devices that can be accessed by many people.

    b) A computer that performs a service on behalf of other network components.

    ((c)) A group of computers that are connected together to communicate and share resources.

    d) A computer with a network operating system.

2. What are the basic network components?

    ((a)) Nodes or workstations

    b) Network adapter

    c) Cable or other network medium

    d) Network resources

    e) Network operating system

3. True or False? A network must contain a group of at least ten or more computers connected together.

    ___ True

    _X_ False

4. Match the network model with its description.

    _C_ Centralized network   a. A network in which some nodes act as servers to provide special services on behalf of other nodes.

    _a_ Client-server network   b. A network in which resource sharing, processing, and communication controls are completely decentralized.

    _b_ Peer-to-peer network   c. A network in which a central computer controls all network communication and performs data processing and storage on behalf of clients.

TOPIC B
Browse Websites with Internet Explorer 8

You have familiarized yourself with the basic components of a computer network. Now, you are ready to familiarize yourself with the basics of the Internet and then start browsing for the Internet resources. In this topic, you will browse websites with Internet Explorer 8.

You obviously need an interface to browse contents and access resources. Windows 7 provides you with Internet Explorer 8, one of the most powerful and widely used browsers available today. Developing your browsing skills will allow you to use the Internet effectively.

The Internet

Definition:

The *Internet* is a computer network that is formed by the interconnection of other computers and networks across the globe. It is the biggest public network in the world and enables users to chat, send and receive email, and share and find data in any location. The Internet provides services such as discussion forums, newsgroups, online shopping, and email. To access the Internet, you need to have an Internet connection and a web browser.

Example:

Figure 6-2: Users connected to the Internet.

The Internet Vs. the Web

Although people use the terms interchangeably, you should know that the Internet and the web are really two different entities. The Internet that has been around in some form for nearly 40 years, is a global public network that provides a variety of services. You can think of the Internet as a massive collection of connected hardware. The web is a particular category of Internet services, and was developed in the 1980s to provide a cataloging system for data stored on the Internet. Unlike the Internet, the web's primary function is not to connect networks, but rather to connect or link, related information by using specific software technologies. You can think of the web as a massive collection of connected information. "Online" and "cyberspace" are the other terms that are often used when referring to the Internet.

Web Addresses

A *web address* is the address of a resource on the Internet. It is also referred to as the *Uniform Resource Locator (URL)*. Every single resource on the web has its own URL. URLs are structured as *protocol://domainname/path/filename*. The protocol, generally "http," identifies the type of application needed to access information. The domain name is usually the name of the company or organization that is hosting the information you want to see. The path shows the directory where the file resides on the host's computer. And, the file name is the actual name and file extension of the file that you want to see.

To view the resource referred to in a web address, you can type the URL either in the **Search programs and files** text box on the **Start** menu or in the address bar of your web browser. You can also click a link that is associated with the URL. The browser will then display that resource.

Figure 6-3: The components of a web address.

Web Browsers

Definition:

A *web browser* is a software application that displays web pages on the Internet. When connected to the Internet, the browser can be used as an interface to access email, discussion forums, online communities, and various other resources. A browser generally consists of a content window along with buttons, an address bar, toolbars, and add-ons. These elements help you navigate to various web pages and view their contents. A browser can also be customized to suit your browsing preferences.

Example:

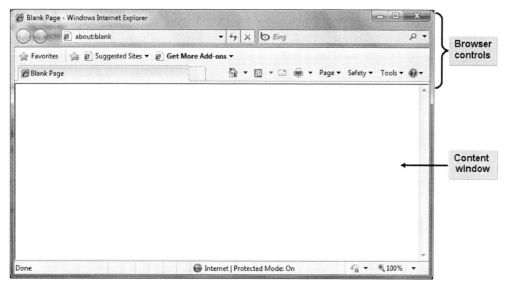

Figure 6-4: A web browser displaying its components.

Websites

Definition:

A *website* is a collection of related web pages that consist of text, pictures, and graphics. A website may contain information on numerous subjects. The default page of a website is called the *home page*. Typically, all pages in a website can be accessed from the site's home page. Web pages are linked together by special pieces of text called *hyperlinks,* which you can click to move directly to different pages or resources on the web. Most hyperlinks appear underlined or in a different color. Pictures may also contain hyperlinks. When you place the mouse pointer over a hyperlink, the mouse pointer changes to a hand shaped pointer. Clicking the hyperlink, whether text or picture, automatically takes you to the linked page.

Example:

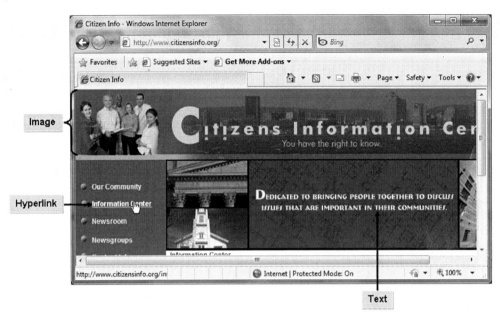

Figure 6-5: A website displaying its various components.

Internet Explorer 8

Internet Explorer 8, popularly referred to as IE 8, is the default browser in Windows 7. Similar to all web browsers, it gives you access to a wide variety of Internet services. With Internet Explorer 8, you can browse web pages and access Internet tools quickly. Simple tools and buttons in this browser enable you to navigate through web pages, and high-level security features protect both your data and privacy from possible online threats. Your online transactions are secure because Internet Explorer 8 can detect malicious websites and prevent information theft.

The Internet Explorer 8 User Interface

The user interface of Internet Explorer 8 has various components that help you when browsing the Internet.

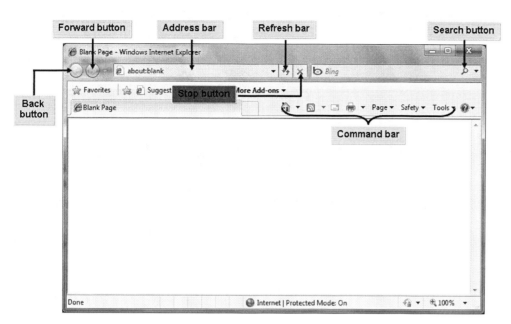

Figure 6-6: The user interface of Internet Explorer 8.

The following table describes the interface elements displayed by default in the Internet Explorer window.

Component	Description
The **Back** and **Forward** buttons	The **Back** button takes you to the previously visited page while the **Forward** button takes you to the next page.
The address bar	Enables you to enter the web address. In Internet Explorer 8, when you enter the address, it tries to complete the address based on the history of your browsing sessions. The matching addresses are displayed in a drop-down list and the matching words are highlighted in blue. After the URL is entered, the domain name of the website is highlighted, thereby enabling users to identify which website they are in.
The **Go/Refresh** button	Connects you to an address typed in the address bar. Once you are connected to a web page, the **Go** button becomes the **Refresh** button.
	The **Refresh** button reloads information on the currently displayed web page.
The **Stop** button	Stops the current web page from loading or reloading.
The **Favorites** bar	Contains favorite links, feeds, and web slices.
Instant Search	Enables you to type a search keyword.
The command bar	Contains frequently used buttons.
The **Display** area	Displays the content of a web page.

Component	Description
The status bar	Displays information about the progress of a program, and indicates the security settings of Internet Explorer 8.

Bing

Bing is a search engine that enables you to search for information, images, and news on the Internet. This service is provided by Microsoft and is set as the default search provider in Internet Explorer 8. The Bing home page consists of the **EXPLORE** pane that provides links to images, videos, shopping, news, maps, and travel information. The hotspots available on the page display factual information and provide links related to the facts. Additional features in the search engine include auto suggestions to search queries, instant answers within search results, best match results, related searches, quick preview of search results, video previews, and Quick Tabs. Bing helps users make informed decisions on subjects such as shopping and travel by providing instant answers for searches in a few mouse clicks.

Tabbed Browsing

Internet Explorer 8 enables you to view multiple web pages on different tabs within a single browser window. Referred to as *tabbed browsing,* this feature enables you to easily switch between web pages. You can open web pages on a new tab either by clicking the **New Tab** button or by double-clicking the tab row. In addition, you can view web pages on a new tab either by choosing the **Open Link in New Tab** option from the shortcut menu or by choosing **File→New Tab.** On a new tab, you can view a previously opened web page by selecting it from the **Reopen closed tabs** section. You can also view your previous browsing session by clicking the **Reopen Last Browsing Session** link.

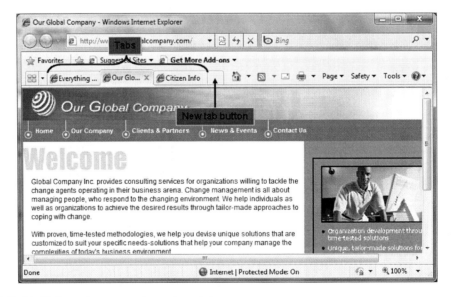

Figure 6-7: Multiple web pages viewed as tabs.

How to Browse Websites with Internet Explorer 8

Procedure Reference: Browse the Web

To browse the web:

1. Ensure that you are connected to the Internet.
2. Launch Internet Explorer 8.
   - Choose **Start→Internet.**
   - Or, on the **Start** menu, choose **All Programs→Internet Explorer.**
3. In the address bar, type an address and press **Enter** to visit the website.
4. View the displayed details.
5. In the navigation pane, use an option to navigate through the web pages.
   - Click the **Back** button to go back to the previously visited web page.
   - Click the **Forward** button to go to the next page that you visited.
   - Click the **Refresh** button to reload a page.
   - Click the **Stop** button to interrupt the transfer of information.
6. If necessary, navigate through the web pages to look for additional information.
   - Click a hyperlink to access an associated resource.
   - On the command bar, click the **Home** button to return to your browser's default home page.

Procedure Reference: Browse Web Pages on Multiple Tabs

To browse web pages on multiple tabs:

1. Open a new tab.
   - On the command bar, double-click an empty location to open a new tab.
   - On the command bar, click the **New Tab** button.
   - Or, press **Ctrl+T.**
2. In the address bar, type the address of the web page and press **Enter.**
3. If necessary, right-click a hyperlink and choose **Open Link in New Tab** to view the associated resource on a new tab.
4. If necessary, view the open tabs in the **Quick Tabs** view.
   a. Click the **Quick Tabs** button to view the open tabs in thumbnail view.
   b. Select the desired thumbnail display of a web page to view its corresponding content.

Clicking the **Quick Tabs** button again closes the **Quick Tabs** view and takes you back to the normal view. You can also click the **Tab List** button and select a tab to view its corresponding web pages.

Procedure Reference: Reopen a Previously Viewed Web Page on a New Tab

To reopen a previously viewed web page on a new tab:

1. Open a new tab.
2. In the **Reopen closed tabs** section, select the web page that you want to view.

Procedure Reference: Search for Information Using Bing

To search for information using **Bing:**

1. Open Internet Explorer 8.
2. At the top-right corner of the Internet Explorer 8 window, in the Internet Explorer search text box, type the desired search term.
3. If necessary, refine your search using search operators.
4. Click the **Search** button to display the search results page that contains the URLs of various web pages related to your query.
5. If necessary, click on a link that matches your query to go to that website.

ACTIVITY 6-2

Browsing with Internet Explorer 8

Before You Begin:
Ensure that you are connected to the Internet.

Scenario:
You want to prepare a presentation at your office for which you need to get some information from the **http://www.citizensinfo.org** and **http://www.ourglobalcompany.com** websites.

What You Do	How You Do It
1. Display multiple web pages on tabs.	a. On the taskbar, click the **Internet Explorer** icon.
	b. If necessary, maximize the Internet Explorer window.
	c. In the address bar, type *www.everythingforcoffee.com* and then press **Enter** to open the website.
	d. Close the yellow colored information bar located below the command bar.
	e. On the tab row, click the **New Tab** button.
	f. In the address bar, type *www.ourglobalcompany.com* and press **Enter** to open the website on a separate tab.
2. View web pages using the **Quick Tabs** view.	a. On the tab row, click the **Quick Tabs** button to view the tabs as thumbnails.
	b. Click the **Quick Tabs** button to return to the **Our Global Company** web page.
	c. Close the **Our Global Company** tab.

3. Search the web for information on change management.

   a. At the top-right corner of the **Everything For Coffee - Windows Internet Explorer** window, in the Internet Explorer search text box, click and type *Change Man*

   b. From the **Bing Suggestions** drop-down list, select **change management.**

   c. In the Internet Explorer search text box, click after "management," and click again to deselect the text and then press the **Spacebar.**

   d. Type *+ "our global company"*

   e. Click the **Search** button to display the search results page.

   f. If necessary, in the **AutoComplete** dialog box, click **No.**

   g. In the list of search results, click the first **Our Global Company** link to view the web page.

DISCOVERY ACTIVITY 6-3
Getting Familiar with the Internet

Scenario:
Your day-to-day tasks require you to find information on the Internet. You decide to familiarize yourself with the basic concepts and functionality of the Internet.

---

1. What is the basic requirement for you to access the Internet?

    (a) Internet connection
    b) Email
    c) Chat
    d) Hyperlinks

2. Which option denotes the correct structure of an URL?

    a) protocol://path/domainname/filename
    (b) protocol://domainname/path/filename
    c) protocol://domainname/filename/path
    d) domainname://protocol/path/filename

3. True or False? A web page may consist of both animations and pictures.

    X True
    __ False

4. What do you call a collection of related web pages?

    a) Home page
    b) Web browser
    (c) Website
    d) Hyperlink

5. True or False? The Quick Tabs feature allows you to open a web page in a new window.

    __ True
    X False

Lesson 6 Follow-up

In this lesson, you browsed the Internet using Internet Explorer 8. On the Internet, you can find information, and send and receive email. Browsing the Internet also helps you understand what cyberspace is all about.

1. **In what ways will the use of the Internet benefit you and your organization?**

2. **In your opinion, which of the features in Internet Explorer 8 will enhance your browsing experience? Why?**

Follow-up

In this course, you acquired the necessary skills and information you will need to understand the basic operations of a personal computer and to work effectively with it. You familiarized yourself with the Windows 7 operating system and acquired the necessary skills to customize the Windows 7 desktop and manage files and folders. You worked with simple tools such as WordPad, Calculator, and Paint and also browsed the Internet. With these basic computing skills, you are prepared to perform a variety of general computing tasks that will help you meet both business requirements and personal computing needs.

1. **What tasks that you perform manually can be performed using a PC?**

2. **How do you think you can use the features of Windows 7 to help you improve your work productivity?**

What's Next?

Microsoft® Windows® 7 Level 1 (First Look) will be the second course in this series.

Microsoft® Windows® 7 Level 2 (First Look) will be the third course in this series.

Lesson Labs

Due to classroom setup constraints, some labs cannot be keyed in sequence immediately following their associated lesson. Your instructor will tell you whether your labs can be practiced immediately following the lesson or whether they require separate setup from the main lesson content.

Introduction to Personal Computers Using Windows® 7

Lesson 1 Lab 1

Buying a New Computer

Activity Time: 5 minutes

Scenario:
You have decided to buy a new computer, which you will be using to type notes for a research paper that you are working on. You also want to ensure that the design configuration serves your purpose. As part of the design specification, you need to decide on the hardware components that you might require to aid your work.

1. You need to take down notes while traveling. In your opinion, what type of personal computer will serve the intended purpose?

   laptop

2. If you were to choose a personal computer that can act as your personal address book and calendar when you travel, which one will you choose?

   a) Desktop
   b) Notebook
   (c) Handheld
   d) Mainframe

3. What hardware enhancement will you suggest for improving the performance of your computer?

   memory

4. Given your requirements, what kind of peripherals do you think that you might need to attach to your computer?

   mouse keyboard

Lesson 2 Lab 1

Identifying the Different Components on the Windows 7 Interface

Activity Time: 10 minutes

Before You Begin:
The computer is switched on and the **Welcome** screen is displayed.

Scenario:
You have started working with a computer that is loaded with the Windows 7 operating system. You need to find some support documentation about using the computer mouse. Once done with this task, you intend to secure your system to prevent unauthorized access.

1. Log on to the computer.

2. Launch the **Windows Help and Support** feature.

3. Search help resources for the documentation on using the mouse.

4. Find and read the documentation on using the keyboard.

5. Close all windows and lock the system.

6. If necessary, unlock the system.

Introduction to Personal Computers Using Windows® 7

Lesson 3 Lab 1

Organizing Folders and Files

Activity Time: 20 minutes

Data Files:

My company details.zip

Before You Begin:

Display the **Windows Explorer** window.

Scenario:

You are getting ready for a conference in which you will be accessing files from the Official folder. For better management during the conference, you first decide to rename this folder "Conference." Then, you want to make this folder more accessible by adding it to the **Favorites** list and by sorting its contents based on their tags. You also need to locate an image file on expense analysis and you know this file is less than 200 kilobytes in size. You want to save the search results, and finally you decide to discard the Accounts folder.

1. Navigate to the C:\084705Data folder using the breadcrumb links.

2. Navigate back to the My company details folder.

3. Rename the Official folder as "Conference."

4. Add the Conference folder to the **Favorites** list.

5. Search for files that contain the word "team" and using search filters, locate the Relocation Team.rtf file.

6. Save the search.

7. Delete the Accounts folder permanently from the system.

Lesson 4 Lab 1

Working with Simple Applications in Windows 7

Activity Time: 10 minutes

Data Files:

Letter to e.Quiry ltd.rtf, Laptop logo.jpg

Before You Begin:

The Windows 7 desktop is displayed.

Scenario:

You are Cary Cook, the marketing manager of Rudison Technologies, a company that sells laptops. A client has placed an order and also asked for the prices of laptops. You want to draft a reply to the client.

- The letter should be formatted in such a way that it looks professional.
- The total price of the requested number of laptops should be entered in the letter.
- The company logo along with the company name should be inserted below your signature.

1. Navigate to the C:\084705Data folder and open the Letter to e.Quiry ltd.rtf file in WordPad.

2. Type **Cary Cook** at the end of the letter and below the name, type your job title as **Marketing Manager.**

3. Calculate the total price using the **Calculator** application and copy it to the WordPad document.

4. Open the Laptop logo.jpg file in Paint.

5. Edit the Laptop logo.jpg file in Paint by adding the company name, **Rudison Technologies.**

6. Save the edited logo as **My_laptop logo.jpg.**

7. Paste the edited logo below your job title in the WordPad document.

8. Save the file as **My_letter to e.Quiry ltd** and close all the open applications.

Introduction to Personal Computers Using Windows® 7

Lesson 5 Lab 1

Customizing the Windows 7 Desktop

Activity Time: 5 minutes

Before You Begin:
The Windows 7 desktop is displayed.

Scenario:
As the manager of an organization, you need to make a client presentation using a computer that has Windows 7 installed on it. You want to ensure that all elements of your desktop reflect your company in one way or the other.

1. On the **Start** menu, place the program icons that you will use frequently during the meeting so that you will be able to quickly access them.

2. Set your company logo as the desktop background.

3. Set the 3D text screen saver using your company's byline.

4. Add the gadget that you would require frequently to the desktop.

Lesson 6 Lab 1

Surfing the Internet

Activity Time: 5 minutes

Scenario:
You are just getting used to the Internet and browsing, and you want to try viewing a couple of your favorite websites.

1. Visit two websites of your choice and browse through the web pages.

2. View the websites and links in the **Tabbed** view.

Solutions

Lesson 1

Activity 1-1

1. What do you call the electronic components of a personal computer?

    a) Software

    ✓ b) Hardware

    c) Mainframe

    d) Laptop

2. Identify some of the uses of personal computers that you are aware of. (Choose three.)

    ✓ a) Create and manage data.

    ✓ b) Perform accounting tasks.

    ✓ c) Send an electronic mail message.

    d) Deposit cash in ATM.

3. True or False? A personal computer is sometimes referred to as a minicomputer.

    ___ True

    ✓ False

Activity 1-2

1. John needs a personal computer that is portable so that he can use it at office and at home, when necessary. He might need it for typical office tasks such as accounting, creating letters and reports, and analyzing numeric information. What will you recommend?

    a) Desktop

    ✓ b) Notebook

    c) Handheld

    d) Mainframe

2. Laura needs a personal computer at the office. It needs to be powerful and easy to upgrade because she intends to use it to create and modify graphics. It does not have to be portable. The price is also an issue because she has a budget and she needs to stay within. What will you recommend?

    a) Notebook

    b) Handheld

    ✓ c) Desktop

    d) Minicomputer

3. John needs a personal computer that he can carry with him wherever he goes. He does a lot of traveling, so it needs to be small and light enough. What will you recommend?

    a) Supercomputer

    b) Desktop

    c) Mainframe computer

    ✓ d) Handheld

Activity 1-3

1. Jim has purchased a new laptop. Which input device will he use?

    a) Mouse

    b) Touchscreen

    ✓ c) Trackball

    d) Joystick

2. Laura wants to type a letter. Which device in the computer will help her do her work?

    a) Monitor

    b) Trackball

    ✓ c) Keyboard

    d) Touchscreen

3. Laura wants to save her family photographs on the computer. Which device will she use to digitalize them first?

    ✓ a) Scanner

    b) Printer

    c) Monitor

    d) Mouse

4. True or False? Jim is interested in flight stimulator games. He is sure that he can play the game using a touchscreen.

    ___ True

    ✓ False

5. **What are the advantages of using a USB device? (Choose two.)**

   a) You can touch up digital photos.

   b) You can insert the device to read hard copy text and translate the information into an electronic form the computer can use.

   ✓ c) You can copy or move data between the USB device and the personal computer.

   ✓ d) You can plug and unplug the device without rebooting the operating system.

Activity 1-4

1. **Identify the devices that you feel will most directly aid Jim in his job as a photographer. (Choose two.)**

   ✓ a) Scanner

   ✓ b) Printer

   c) Joystick

   d) Keyboard

2. **True or False? The video card in Jim's computer enables him to view images on the monitor.**

   ✓ True

   ___ False

3. **Laura needs to print inventory lists on a regular basis, but overall quality is not important. Which printer must she use?**

   a) The laser printer

   b) The inkjet printer

   ✓ c) The dot-matrix printer

   d) The copy machine

4. **Jim needs to print reports with high quality text and graphics. Which printers can he use? (Choose two.)**

   a) The dot-matrix printer

   ✓ b) The laser printer

   ✓ c) The inkjet printer

   d) The copy machine

Activity 1-5

1. **Jim is a photographer. He needs to copy his work onto a storage medium that has a minimum capacity of 100 MB and distribute his photos to clients. Which device will you recommend to accomplish this?**

   a) Floppy drive

   ✓ b) CD-RW drive

   c) DVD drive

   d) Joystick

2. Which storage device is rewritable and capable of storing a fairly large amount of data?

   a) CD-ROM

   b) Floppy disk

   ✓ c) USB flash drive

   d) CD-W

3. True or False? The operating system needed to start Jim's computer is stored in the computer hard disk.

   ✓ True

   ___ False

Activity 1-6

1. John is searching for a proper place to keep the computer. What will be your suggestion?

   a) Placing the computer on an existing file cabinet.

   b) Using a wheeled table.

   c) Placing the computer near a window so that there is good ventilation.

   ✓ d) Locating the computer in a spare room.

2. John experiences back pain from arching his neck while viewing the monitor. How could he alleviate the problem? (Choose three.)

   ✓ a) Place the monitor at eye level.

   ✓ b) Use a chair which gives support to the lower back.

   c) Rest his head on the chair while working.

   ✓ d) Place the monitor at a distance of 9-12 inches.

3. True or False? Ergonomics is the study of the problems of people in adjusting to their environment.

   ✓ True

   ___ False

4. True or False? By keeping a good posture and using proper equipment, John can avoid RSI.

   ✓ True

   ___ False

Activity 1-7

1. **Jim has been advised to restart his computer whenever a new application program is installed on his computer. What is the first thing that happens when Jim restarts the computer?**

    a) The computer loads other basic software.

    ✓ b) The computer performs a series of self-tests and diagnostics.

    c) The computer loads the operating system.

    d) The computer shuts down automatically.

2. **Where does the computer store the new software that Jim has loaded?**

    ✓ a) In the hard drive

    b) In the RAM

    c) In the ROM

    d) In computer memory

3. **True or False? The critical data required for booting a computer is stored in the ROM.**

    ✓ True

    ___ False

4. **True or False? Jim's computer has 40 GB memory when compared to his colleague's computer memory which is 20 GB. The performance and capabilities of Jim's computer will be better than his colleague's computer.**

    ✓ True

    ___ False

Lesson 1 Follow-up

Lesson 1 Lab 1

1. **You need to take down notes while traveling. In your opinion, what type of personal computer will serve the intended purpose?**

    You need a personal computer that is portable. A laptop will be the best fit for this situation.

2. **If you were to choose a personal computer that can act as your personal address book and calendar when you travel, which one will you choose?**

    a) Desktop

    b) Notebook

    ✓ c) Handheld

    d) Mainframe

3. **What hardware enhancement will you suggest for improving the performance of your computer?**

   The more memory a PC has, the greater the computer's performance and capabilities. This will ensure that your applications open up quickly.

4. **Given your requirements, what kind of peripherals do you think that you might need to attach to your computer?**

   Because you do a lot of documentation, you might need a printer to take printouts of important documents. You might also need a scanner to quickly scan documents and illustrations for future use.

Lesson 2

Activity 2-3

1. **Which elements are displayed on the Windows 7 Welcome screen?**
   - ✓ a) The Shut down options menu
   - b) The recently used programs
   - ✓ c) The user logon options
   - ✓ d) The Ease of access button
   - e) The Start button

2. **Which option allows you to change the accessibility settings before logging on to your computer?**
   - a) The Switch User option
   - b) The Shut down options menu
   - ✓ c) The Ease of Access option
   - d) The Logon text box

3. **What will be the appropriate mouse action to display a shortcut menu?**
   - a) Click
   - ✓ b) Right-click
   - c) Double-click
   - d) Drag

Activity 2-5

1. **Which among the following is a container object?**
   - a) Shortcut to C disk drive
   - b) A word document file
   - ✓ c) The C disk drive
   - d) A pop-up description of a program

2. Which elements are found on the Start menu?

    ✓ a) The Shut down options

    ✓ b) The link to Control Panel

    c) The Show Desktop option

    ✓ d) A list of recently used files

    ✓ e) Frequently accessed programs

Activity 2-7

1. Which window component displays additional information about the buttons, commands, and processes in the window?

    a) The menu bar

    b) The toolbar

    ✓ c) The status bar

    d) The title bar

2. Which feature is used to display an active window and minimize all the other open windows?

    a) Aero Flip

    b) Snap

    c) Aero Peek

    ✓ d) Shake

Activity 2-9

1. Which option enables you to locate content on the displayed help page?

    a) The More on the Windows website link

    b) The Search Help text box

    ✓ c) The Options button on the navigation bar

    d) The Browse Help button on the navigation bar

2. Which button on the navigation bar enables you to seek help from a Microsoft support professional or to use a Windows website forum?

    ✓ a) The Ask button

    b) The Help and Support home button

    c) The Options button

    d) The Browse Help button

Activity 2-10

2. **Under which of these situations will you restart a computer?**

    a) When another user has to log on to the system

    ✓ b) When a program is not responding to your commands

    c) When the system is to be awakened from its Sleep state

    d) When a day's work is done

    ✓ e) When a program is installed on your computer

Activity 2-11

1. **You have a meeting to attend and your colleague will also attend the meeting with you. However, you will return to your workstation within a short while and resume your current working session. Which power option will you choose?**

    a) The Log off option

    ✓ b) The Lock option

    c) The Switch user option

    d) The Shut down option

2. **What happens when a system is in the Sleep state?**

    ✓ a) All open documents are saved, applications remain in the same state, and the system moves into a paused state.

    b) Your working session gets terminated.

    c) All open applications are closed and the system moves into a paused state.

    d) The user is prompted to save files and the system moves into a paused state.

Lesson 3

Activity 3-2

1. **Which sections are not displayed by default in Windows Explorer? (Choose two.)**

    a) The command bar

    ✓ b) The preview pane

    c) The details pane

    ✓ d) The menu bar

    e) The address bar

2. Where can you view file information and add properties to a file?

   a) The address bar

   ✓ b) The details pane

   c) The preview pane

   d) The navigation pane

Activity 3-5

1. Which option deletes files permanently from the system?

   a) Delete

   ✓ b) Empty Recycle Bin

   c) Restore

   d) Create a Shortcut

2. True or False? The Favorites list provides a shortcut to the user's desktop.

   ✓ True

   __ False

Activity 3-7

1. You have selected a sample picture that you want to burn to a CD. Which option will you choose to display the Burn a Disc wizard to begin the CD burning process?

   a) Burn→DVD.

   b) Burn→CD.

   c) File→Burn.

   ✓ d) Burn→Data Disc.

2. True or False? You can make a backup of your files only from your computer to a removable storage device such as a CD.

   __ True

   ✓ False

Lesson 4

Activity 4-1

1. James wants to type a letter and send it to a client. Which application will be best suited for this job?

   a) A spreadsheet

   b) A database

   ✓ c) A word processor

   d) Presentation software

2. After typing the letter, James wants to modify the company logo and insert it in the letter. Which application can he use for this work?

    a) A word processor

    b) A database

    c) Presentation software

    ✓ d) A graphics application

3. True or False? James needs to prepare handouts containing charts and bulleted lists. He can accomplish this using a spreadsheet application.

    ___ True

    ✓ False

4. James needs to record and maintain a list of clients' names, contact details, price quotations, and other details related to transactions. Which application software will you recommend to accomplish this task?

    a) A web browser

    b) A word processor

    ✓ c) A database

    d) Presentation software

Activity 4-3

1. Which tab in the WordPad window lets you copy, paste, format, edit, and insert elements in a document?

    ✓ a) Home

    b) View

    c) Format

    d) Insert

2. True or False? By default, the Quick Access toolbar is located below the WordPad Ribbon.

    ___ True

    ✓ False

Activity 4-5

1. Which button will you press to clear the current calculation in the Calculator?

    a) The MR button

    ✓ b) The C button

    c) The Backspace button

    d) The = button

2. Which button will you press to clear the Calculator's memory?

   a) The C button

   ✓ b) The MC button

   c) The Backspace button

   d) The = button

Activity 4-7

1. Which group in the Paint window contains the Text tool?

   a) Clipboard

   b) Shapes

   c) Image

   ✓ d) Tools

2. True or False? You can adjust the size and thickness of a shape inserted in the Paint window.

   ✓ True

   ___ False

Lesson 5

Activity 5-2

1. Which option on the Start menu enables you to add programs to it so that you can access the added programs quickly and easily?

   a) Add to Start Menu

   ✓ b) Pin to Start Menu

   c) Default Programs

   d) Properties

2. True or False? The Pin to Start Menu option enables you to add a program icon to the frequently used program section of the Start menu.

   ___ True

   ✓ False

Activity 5-4

1. **Which option in the Taskbar and Start Menu Properties dialog box hides the taskbar automatically when not in use?**

    a) Lock the taskbar

    ✓ b) Auto-hide the taskbar

    c) Taskbar buttons

    d) Taskbar location on screen

2. **Identify the options in the Taskbar and Start Menu Properties dialog box for customizing the taskbar.**

    ✓ a) Taskbar buttons

    ✓ b) Notification area

    ✓ c) Preview desktop with Aero Peek

    d) Task Manager

Activity 5-6

1. **Which option will you choose from the desktop right-click menu to arrange icons in alphabetical order?**

    ✓ a) Sort by→Name.

    b) Sort by→Size.

    c) Sort by→Item type.

    d) Sort by→Date modified.

2. **True or False? It is possible to specify a color for your desktop background instead of an image.**

    ✓ True

    ___ False

Activity 5-8

1. **What does the Wait option in the Screen Saver Settings dialog box denote?**

    ✓ a) The idle time after which the screen saver gets activated.

    b) The time for which the screen saver is displayed.

    c) The time interval between two screen saver sessions.

    d) The time after which the next screen saver option is activated.

2. **True or False? Screen savers are primarily used to prevent people passing by from seeing what is on your computer screen.**

    ✓ True

    ___ False

Activity 5-10

1. What are the default gadgets available in the Windows 7 Gadgets gallery?
   - ✓ a) Clock
   - b) Traffic Update
   - ✓ c) Weather
   - ✓ d) Feed Headlines

2. True or False? All the gadgets are provided with customization options.
   - ___ True
   - ✓ False

Lesson 6

Activity 6-1

1. What is a computer network?
   - a) A set of hardware devices that can be accessed by many people.
   - b) A computer that performs a service on behalf of other network components.
   - ✓ c) A group of computers that are connected together to communicate and share resources.
   - d) A computer with a network operating system.

2. What are the basic network components?
   - ✓ a) Nodes or workstations
   - ✓ b) Network adapter
   - ✓ c) Cable or other network medium
   - d) Network resources
   - ✓ e) Network operating system

3. True or False? A network must contain a group of at least ten or more computers connected together.
   - ___ True
   - ✓ False

4. Match the network model with its description.

_c_	Centralized network	a.	A network in which some nodes act as servers to provide special services on behalf of other nodes.
_a_	Client-server network	b.	A network in which resource sharing, processing, and communication controls are completely decentralized.
_b_	Peer-to-peer network	c.	A network in which a central computer controls all network communication and performs data processing and storage on behalf of clients.

Activity 6-3

1. **What is the basic requirement for you to access the Internet?**

    ✓ a) Internet connection

    b) Email

    c) Chat

    d) Hyperlinks

2. **Which option denotes the correct structure of an URL?**

    a) protocol://path/domainname/filename

    ✓ b) protocol://domainname/path/filename

    c) protocol://domainname/filename/path

    d) domainname://protocol/path/filename

3. **True or False? A web page may consist of both animations and pictures.**

    ✓ True

    __ False

4. **What do you call a collection of related web pages?**

    a) Home page

    b) Web browser

    ✓ c) Website

    d) Hyperlink

5. **True or False? The Quick Tabs feature allows you to open a web page in a new window.**

    __ True

    ✓ False

Glossary

Aero effect
A scheme that provides a rich visual experience with a glossy and transparent user interface.

Aero Peek feature
A feature that is used to display the desktop among a lot of windows by making the open windows transparent.

Bing
A search engine provided by Microsoft that enables you to search for information, images, and news on the Internet.

bit map
A representation consisting of rows and columns of dots of a digital image in computer memory.

bit
The smallest unit of information on a computer system. Bit is short for binary digit represented either as 1 or 0.

boot process
The process of starting or restarting your computer by loading the operating system from the computer's hard drive.

boot
The process of starting the computer. Short for bootstrap.

byte
A unit of computer storage equal to approximately one character.

Calculator
A program similar to a handheld calculator that is used for solving math problems.

CD-ROM
A compact disc stamped by the vendor that cannot be erased and filled with new data.

CD-RW
A re-recordable disc that lets you record a CD, then write new data over the already recorded data.

CD-W
An optical disc that is used to store digital data. Data cannot be overwritten once it is recorded to the disc.

centralized network
A network in which a central computer controls all network communication and performs data processing and storage on behalf of clients.

client-server network
A network in which computer functionality is divided into two roles: servers and clients.

client
The computers that use network services.

Close
A button on the title bar that is used to close a window.

cold boot
The process of turning off the power and then turning the machine back on.

computer cards
The cards that enable computers to perform certain specific functions that increase the capability of a computer.

computer network
A group of computers that are connected together.

computer
A machine that stores, retrieves, and processes data.

container
A container that allows you to store files as well as other containers.

control keys
The keys on the keyboard that provide cursor and screen control.

CPU
(Central Processing Unit) A tiny electronic chip within the system unit.

CTS
(Carpal Tunnel Syndrome) A painful disorder caused by a buildup of tissue in the nerve channels of the hands and wrists.

cursor
A symbol on the screen indicating where the text or graphics will be inserted or erased.

cycle
The smallest unit of time recognized by a PC.

data backup
A process of copying files from one location on your computer to a different location or to a removable storage device, such as a floppy disk, CD, or DVD.

data input
The stage in which you issue commands or enter information into the software.

data
An input such as information that is entered, stored, or processed in a computer.

desktop background
The actual appearance of the desktop itself, usually a picture or a color.

desktop
A type of personal computer that is designed for use on your desk at home or in an office.

desktop
The work area where dialog boxes, windows, icons, and menus appear.

disk drive
A peripheral device that is used to permanently store and retrieve information.

domain name
A part of the URL that is usually the name of the company or organization that is hosting the information you want to see.

dot-matrix printers
The printers that create characters by striking pins against an ink ribbon. Each pin makes a dot, and combinations of dots form characters and illustrations.

DVD-ROM
A read-only compact disc having the capacity to hold 4.7 GB to 17 GB.

Ease of access button
A button that allows users with disabilities to set accessibility options to navigate easily within the operating system.

Ergonomics
The study of the problems of people in adjusting to their environment, especially the science that seeks to adapt work and working conditions to suit a worker.

file extensions
The format of a file and its type that is used to identify the program that is associated with the file.

file name
A part of the URL that is the actual name and file extension of the file that you want to see.

file
A collection of data that is stored under a single name.

floppy disk
A data storage medium composed of a thin, flexible disk and having a storage capacity of 1.4 MB.

folder and file properties
The pieces of information about a file or folder, other than its content, that are stored with the file.

folder
A container object that contains files and folders in an organized manner.

function keys
The keys on the computer keyboard that can be programmed to perform certain actions.

gadget
An application that is programmed to provide specific information.

Gadgets gallery
A gallery that displays the list of default gadgets available in Windows 7.

gigahertz
The measurement of the CPU's speed in billions of cycles per second.

handheld
A type of personal computer that is designed to fit in your hands, and can be carried wherever you go.

hard disk
A fixed component within the computer that is used to permanently store information.

hardware
The electronic and mechanical components of a personal computer such as the monitor, keyboard, mouse, processor, motherboard, network card, and so on.

home page
The default page in a website.

hyperlink
A special text or picture that you can click to move directly to different pages or resources on the web.

inkjet printers
The printers that spray ink at a sheet of paper; produce high-quality text and graphics.

Internet Explorer 8
The default browser in Windows 7 that gives you access to a wide variety of Internet services.

Internet
A global public network that is formed by the interconnection of other computers and networks across the globe.

joystick
A lever that moves in all directions and controls the movement of a pointer or some other display symbol.

jump list
A list of menu options related to a program or application that is displayed on the taskbar and Start menu.

keyboard
An input device that is made up of individual keys presented in a standard arrangement of characters representing individual number, letters, and symbols.

laptop
A type of portable personal computer that can either be plugged in or run on battery.

laser printers
The printers that work similar to copy machines, and produce high-quality printouts quietly and quickly.

library
A container used to manage documents, music, pictures, and other files stored on a computer.

Lock option
An option that enables you to secure your working session if you need to leave your computer for a short period of time.

Log Off option
An option that enables you to end your working session without turning off the computer.

mainframe
A type of computer frequently used to run multiple programs at the same time that can support hundreds or thousands of users simultaneously.

Maximize/Restore
A button on the title bar that is used to expand the active window's screen, and restore the screen from its expanded state to its previous size.

megahertz
The measurement of the CPU's speed in millions of cycles per second.

memory
The power dependent area within the computer that stores information.

menu bar
A window component that contains several menus, that in turn, display their commands.

minicomputer
A type of computer that can support from four to hundreds of users simultaneously.

Minimize
A button on the title bar that is used to reduce a window to a button on the taskbar.

modem
A computer hardware that enables the PC to connect to the Internet and transmit data over telephone lines.

monitor
A peripheral that enables users to view text and graphical data associated with a computer program.

motherboard
The main circuit board of the computer.

mouse
A small handheld input device that is used for moving the cursor on the computer screen.

network card
A component that extends a computer's capabilities to enable it to communicate with other computers and devices on a network.

notification area
An area that displays system related notifications and links to system settings. It is located at the bottom-right corner of the taskbar.

numeric keypad
The set of keys on the right of the keyboard; works like a calculator.

object attributes
An object's properties that are specific and unique to the object.

object
A basic component in Windows 7 represented by small pictures called icons.

OS
(Operating System) Software that acts as an interface between the computer hardware and the application programs that you install on your computer.

Paint tool
A graphics program that supplies a variety of tools and colors for creating and modifying your drawings.

password
A case-sensitive string of characters that must be typed before a user can access a computer.

path
A part of the URL that shows the directory where the file resides on the host's computer.

peer-to-peer network
A network in which resource sharing, processing, and communication controls are completely decentralized.

permissions
The security properties that determine access to resources such as files and printers.

personal computer
A small size computer that is designed for an individual user. It is sometimes called a microcomputer or PC.

pixel
A single point in a graphic image.

port
An outlet that is used to connect a component to a PC.

printer
A device that is used to transfer a copy of the information that is either stored on your computer or displayed on your screen onto a sheet of paper.

processing
The stage in which the computer processes data.

protocol
A part of the URL that identifies the type of application needed to access information.

Quick Access toolbar
A toolbar that provides easy access to core commands such as save a document, undo a previous action, and repeat a previous action.

RAM
(random access memory) A set of microchips that temporarily stores information for the CPU to access quickly while the PC is running.

Recycle Bin
A feature that allows you to open, empty, rename, or create a shortcut and view its properties.

resolution
The sharpness and clarity of the images displayed.

Restart option
An option that enables you to reload Windows 7 and refresh the system's memory without turning off the computer or switching it on.

ribbon
A window component that contains several tabs, that in turn, display their commands.

rights
The security settings that control what system-wide actions users can perform on a computer.

ROM
(read-only memory) A memory that has prerecorded data, and retains information even when the PC is switched off.

RSI
(Repetitive Strain Injury) A painful condition associated with doing a particular activity repeatedly or for long periods of time.

scanner
A device that reads hard copy text, or graphs and translates information into an electronic form the computer can use.

screen saver
A slide show of a picture or text that displays on computer screen after a certain period of user inactivity.

server
The computers that provide network services and control network operations.

Shake feature
A feature that allows you to keep the active window visible on screen while minimizing the rest of the open windows.

shortcut
A link that points to another file or container object.

Shut down option
An option that allows you to turn off your system in a secure manner.

Shut Down Options menu
A menu that enables you to apply a power setting to your computer.

Sleep option
An option that puts the system in the power-saving mode.

Snap feature
A feature that resizes a window by a click of the mouse.

software application
A software program that is designed to perform a specific task in the processing of data.

software
A specific set of electronic instructions that a personal computer uses to operate and perform specific functions and tasks. Examples of software include Data Operating System (DOS), Windows 7, Microsoft Office 2010, Paint, WordPad, and so on.

sound card
A component that facilitates the computer to output audio signals through the attached speakers or the headphones.

speaker
An output device that provides an audio output when an audio file is played.

Start menu
A list of commands that allow you to start programs, open recently used files, search for files and programs, adjust computer settings, and perform other tasks.

startup
The process of setting into operation.

status bar
A window component that provides additional information about the buttons, commands, and processes in the window.

storage device
A device to hold data even when the computer is turned off.

submenu
A list of choices that branches out from a main menu.

supercomputer
The fastest computer that is often used in research and simulation capacities by hospitals, universities, and governments to accomplish a single, specialized task.

SVGA
A set of graphic standards.

Switch User option
An option that enables multiple users to open working sessions on their systems at the same time.

tabbed browsing
A browsing feature available in Internet Explorer 8 in which you can view multiple web pages on different tabs within a single browser window.

taskbar
A rectangular bar located at the bottom of the desktop.

title bar
A window component that displays the program's name and the name of the file currently opened.

touchscreen
A display that can detect the location of touches within the display area.

trackball
A device that is often used with laptop computers; works like an upside-down mouse.

URL
(Uniform Resource Locator) An address of a resource on the Internet.

USB Flash Drive
A compact, removable storage device that plugs into the USB port of a computer in order to transfer information.

USB
(Universal Serial Bus) A standard, compact removable storage device that can be connected to any personal computer to copy or move data between the USB device and the personal computer.

user account
An account that identifies a user to the computer.

user name
A unique name identifying a user account to Windows 7.

video card
A component that interprets information from the processor and sends it to the monitor.

warm boot
The process of restarting a computer that is already turned on.

web address

An address of a resource on the Internet.

web browser

A software application that displays web pages on the Internet.

website

A collection of related web pages.

Windows 7 Welcome screen

A screen that is displayed when you switch on your computer. It allows you to access programs and applications on your system.

Windows Explorer

A tool that offers a single view of all the resources and information that you can access from the computer.

Windows Help and Support

A central location where you can learn how to get things done, solve problems, and obtain product support information.

word processor

A computer application that is used to compose, edit, format, and print text.

WordPad

A simple word-processing application that has basic formatting tools.

Index

A

Aero effects, 60

B

Bing, 170
bit maps, 10
bits, 34
boot, 31
   Also See: startup
boot process, 34
buttons
  Close, 58
  Ease of access, 46
  Maximize/Restore, 58
  Minimize, 58
  Shut down, 52
bytes, 34

C

Calculator, 117
  calculating, 118
CD-ROM, 22
CD-RW, 22
CD-W, 22
clients, 163
cold boot, 42
computer cards, 16
  network, 16
  sound, 16
  video, 16
computer networks, 162
computers, 2
  locking, 72
  shutting down, 72
containers, 53

control keys, 41
CPU, 26
CTS, 28
cursor, 9

D

data, 31
data backup, 100
data input, 31
desktop, 52
  adding or removing common desktop icons, 143
  exploring, 55
desktop background, 142
  changing, 143
desktops, 3
disk drives, 22
domain name, 166

E

Ergonomics, 28

F

features
  Aero Peek, 60
  Shake, 60
  Snap, 60
file and folder naming conventions, 80
file extensions, 79
file name, 166
files, 53, 78
  copying and pasting, 93
  renaming, 92
  saving, 112
floppy disk, 22

folder and file management actions, 89
folder and file properties, 90
folders, 79
  copying and pasting, 93
  navigating, 84
  renaming, 92
function keys, 41

G

gadgets, 154
  displaying, 156
  modifying the gadget options, 156
Gadgets gallery, 155
gigahertz, 26

H

handhelds, 3
hard disk, 24
hardware, 2
home pages, 167
hyperlinks, 167

I

Internet, 165
Internet Explorer 8, 168
  browsing the web, 171

J

joystick, 11
jump lists, 61
  pinning an item, 63

K

keyboards, 9

L

laptops, 3
libraries, 81

M

mainframes, 5
megahertz, 26
memory, 33
menu bar, 58
menus
  adding a program to the Start menu, 131
  customizing the Start Menu properties, 131
  Shut Down Options, 46
  Start, 52

minicomputers, 5
modem, 19
monitors, 15
motherboard, 26
mouse, 9
  moving the mouse, 47
mouse actions, 43
mouse controls, 43

N

notification area, 53
numeric keypad, 41

O

object attributes, 54
objects, 53
options
  Lock, 71
  Log Off, 71
  Restart, 72
  Shut down, 71
  Sleep, 72
  Switch User, 71
OS, 32

P

Paint tool, 122
  modifying a picture, 123
passwords, 44
path, 166
permissions, 44
personal computers, 2
  uses, 6
personalization options, 141
pixels, 15
ports, 27
printers, 17
  dot-matrix, 17
  inkjet, 17
  laser, 17
processing, 31
protocol, 166

Q

Quick Access toolbar, 111

R

RAM, 33

Recycle Bin, 91
  using to delete or restore files or folders, 93
resolution, 15
ribbon, 58
rights, 44
ROM, 33
RSI, 28

S

scanners, 10
screen savers, 149
  setting up, 150
servers, 163
shortcuts, 53
  creating, 94
software, 2
software applications, 106
speakers, 20
startup, 31
  Also See: boot
status bar, 58
storage devices, 22
submenus, 53
supercomputers, 6
SVGA, 15

T

tabbed browsing, 170
taskbar, 52
  changing the location, 136
  customizing, 135
  pinning an item, 136

text selection techniques, 111
title bar, 58
touchscreen, 11
trackball, 11
types of networks
  centralized, 163
  client-server, 163
  peer-to-peer, 163
typing keys, 40

U

URL, 166
USB, 10
USB Flash Drive, 22
user accounts, 44
user names, 44

W

warm boot, 42
web addresses, 166
web browsers, 166
websites, 167
Windows 7 Welcome screen, 45
  configuring the Ease of Access options, 47
Windows Explorer, 80
Windows Explorer components, 82
Windows Help and Support, 67
  accessing, 68
word processors, 108
WordPad, 110
  creating and saving a document, 112
  opening an existing WordPad document, 113

Looking for media files?

They are now conveniently located at www.elementk.com/courseware-file-downloads

Downloading is quick and easy:

1. Visit www.elementk.com/courseware-file-downloads
2. In the search field, type in either the part number or the title
3. Of the courseware titles displayed, choose your title by clicking on the name
4. Links to the data files are located in the middle of the screen
5. Follow the instructions on the screen based upon your web browser

Note that there may be other files available for download in addition to the course files.

Approximate download times:

The amount of time it takes to download your data files will vary according to the file's size and your Internet connection speed. A broadband connection is highly recommended. The average time to download a 10 mb file on a broadband connection is less than 1 minute.